Not Your Mo ... W9-BAJ-369 ...
On Being a Mom

Created by
Dahlynn McKowen,
Ken McKowen and Dianna Graveman

Published by
Publishing Syndicate

PO Box 607
Orangevale California 95662
www.PublishingSyndicate.com

Not Your Mother's Book . . .

On Being a Mom

Copyright 2014 by Publishing Syndicate LLC

*We would like to thank the many individuals
who granted us permission to reprint their stories.
See the complete listing beginning on page 310.*

Created and edited by Dahlynn McKowen,
Ken McKowen and Dianna Graveman
Proofreading by Pat Nelson
Cover and book design by Publishing Syndicate
Cover photo: Creatista/Shutterstock.com

Published by
Publishing Syndicate
PO Box 607
Orangevale California 95662

www.PublishingSyndicate.com
www.Facebook.com/PublishingSyndicate
Twitter: @PublishingSynd

Print Edition ISBN: 978-1-938778-14-8
EPUB Digital Edition ISBN: 978-1-938778-15-5
MOBI Digital Edition ISBN: 978-1-938778-19-2

Library of Congress Control Number 2013907706

Printed in Canada

This book is a collaborative effort. Writers from all over the world submitted their work for consideration, with 64 stories being selected.

Publishing Syndicate strongly encourages you to submit your story for one of its many anthologies. You'll find information on how to do so at the end of this book, starting on page 312.

Dedication

For my mother, Doris:

My mother and I loved each other fiercely and shared an unshakable mother-daughter bond until the end of her life. We also shared a tremendous love for my children—her only grandchildren.

For all of her sacrifices and sleepless nights—not to mention the times I embarrassed her in public—I dedicate this book to her memory . . . but only the stories without "inappropriate language," as she was a very proper lady.

Miss you, Mom.

~~ Dianna Graveman

Doris celebrating her 75th birthday with her daughter Dianna (2009)

Doris and Dianna (1959)

CONTENTS

3 You Just Never Know

4 Yes, I'm Your Mother

5 Day In and Day Out

6 You Did What?!

7 Lessons in Motherhood

8 Letting Go

Acknowledgments

You are all the greatest!

From Dianna:

Thanks to my three great kids—Steve, Beth and Teresa—for years of parenting joy and for loving me in spite of my many mommy mishaps.

Thank you to Don for making me a mommy (I couldn't have done it without you).

Thanks to Donna, Suzanne and Nancy for all the years we spent together navigating the murky waters of motherhood. Grandmotherhood should be a cinch.

And thank you to Linda O'Connell, co-creator of *Not Your Mother's Book. . . On Family*, for making this book's journey to publication so much fun.

From Dahlynn and Ken:

Thank you to Dahlynn's teen son Shawn. Your patience with us as we create another book is much appreciated. We love you!

Thanks to Shayla Seay for your help. You deserve a million gold medals for keeping us organized!

And thank you to Pat Nelson for your excellent proofing skills. We couldn't have done this without you!

And from all of us at Publishing Syndicate:

A special thanks to the many writers who submitted stories for this book. Without you, this book would not have come together like it did. Your stories were wonderful and we thank you for sharing them with us and the world. We only wish we could have printed every story submitted.

Keep those stories coming in for future NYMB titles: www.PublishingSyndicate.com.

Introduction

"A mother is a person who, seeing there are only four pieces of pie for five people, promptly announces she never did care for pie."

~~ Tenneva Jordan

I belong to a family of five, and five can be tricky: somebody has to ride the roller coaster alone while the rest of the family doubles up in seats made for two. Somebody has to forgo the pizza in a pie sliced for eight, so everybody else can have seconds. That someone is usually a mother, and she sacrifices lovingly, with fullness of heart, if not of stomach.

Twenty-nine years ago, I became a mother. I knew nothing about children, and panic quickly set in. Then I had two more children. My panic grew.

But so did my joy.

It hasn't always been easy, and it hasn't always been fun. At times, I felt overwhelmed by the challenges. But always, I felt blessed.

Within this book are stories of moms who have faced the many challenges of motherhood head-on with humor, ingenuity, and occasionally a good wine. From pregnancy police to new-parent jitters, from potty predicaments to school-day debacles, today's moms know how to juggle it all with the aplomb of a high-level executive or a nominee for Volunteer of the Year. Sure, our kids sometimes embarrass us in public, but modern moms take it all in stride, dishing it out as well as they take it. And when the chicks finally leave the nest—some soaring, some tumbling—moms are there to see them off with a hug and a care package and not a small measure of sadness to see them go.

A mother's journey is full of sleepless nights, anxiety-ridden days, years of sacrifice and more love than a heart should conceivably hold. But ask a mother whose kids are grown if she'd do it all again, and the answer will almost certainly be a resounding, "YES!"

Besides, now that they're gone, she can admit she really does like pie.

~~ Dianna Graveman

Challenge
Accepted

On your mark, get set . . .

Kill the Wabbit

by
Georgia Mellie Justad

After spending what was supposedly a "romantic" week in Jamaica with my husband, Todd, I knew something was wrong when I preferred to watch the Atlanta Braves on the TV from commode-side as opposed to sipping rum-runners poolside. I didn't know at the time, but I had the *Exorcist* bit down pat. I only needed to perfect the part of levitating above the bed to give Linda Blair a run for her money. Every time Todd came near me with any ludicrous amorous notions of me performing my "wifely duties," I responded the only way possible—by putting my head into the nearest trash can. Thank God for the nude beach across the bay to take his mind off my racy teddy that served as a barf bib.

"Can't we do something fun, like trying out the hot tub?" he asked, as if I were some hot swimsuit model. He stroked my hair, caked with regurgitated french fries. "I know, let's head down to the beach and try the curried goat on a stick. It smells so good. And then maybe beach limbo."

"Limbo? Seriously?" I asked, as I hurled ginger ale. "Are you forgetting that rousing game of shuffleboard we attempted yesterday followed by the romantic couple's massage?"

"Who could forget? You threw up during both of them," he said with his I'm-so-over-it and when-am-I-getting-laid attitude. Todd turned his attention to the water, straining to see the wildlife on "The Island of Buck-Naked Women" across the bay.

"Why don't you get some binoculars from the front desk and see what's going on over there on boob beach. Better yet, why don't you see if they have any night-vision goggles so you don't miss anything," I retorted.

Chalk it up to luck, as in bad luck. We had been looking forward to this trip for ages and everything was included: tropical flaming drinks—yuck. Curried, exotic food—double yuck. Romantic, rollicking sunset cruises around the bay—forget about it. Had it not been the surprise inclusion of the clothing-optional beach across the bay, Todd said it would have been a total waste of a trip. I had to agree.

Just when I began to actually enjoy watching the baseball game, I considered calling the hotel doctor. I quickly changed my mind, however, after hearing a girl in the lobby discussing her visit with the dreadlocked "witch doctor," whose exams included everything but a live snake, a severed chicken foot and rambling incantations. No thank you, mon.

I flew home facedown, stretched across three seats, fantasizing about getting to my doctor and mercifully being euthanized. Everyone else on the plane—Todd included—sipped free champagne.

As soon as we landed, Todd drove me to the gynecologist's office. He parked the car then headed for the drugstore across the street to have our photos developed. "I think I'll wait for the pictures," he said, smiling. "No point in making another trip over."

That film had nudie beach written all over it. "Yeah, a hundred bucks says you won't be able to walk right after looking at those pictures anyway," I said to him as I headed into the doctor's office, alone.

After a few minutes, I was taken into a small room. "I don't think it is endometriosis this time," said the good doctor after his examination.

"So, what is it?" I demanded. "It can't be my gallbladder. You yanked that out last year."

"A gastrointestinal problem, I think. I know a doctor; tell him I sent you and let me know how it works out," he said, handing me the name of yet another specialist to add to my growing collection.

"A stomach problem? What kind of a stomach problem could cause so much pain and nausea? Maybe it's a tapeworm," I said, as I recalled the many places my head had been in the past few days as the flies circled me. The doctor shook his head and, as he walked out of the room, told me to contact the specialist.

After I made a hysterical call to Mama that evening, she hopped onto a plane the following morning. Then I called my sister Kim, who had her own diagnosis. She told me that I was, as she put it, "knocked up and carrying Rosemary's—wait, Rose-Mellie's—baby." And as for that horrible stomach pain

I had been experiencing, she said it was simply the kicking of tiny cloven hooves against my spleen.

Mama went to the gastroenterologist with me. We learned the only way to find out what was going on in my stomach was to go inside it and have a look around. *Well, why the hell not!* I thought. *Every other doctor in South Florida has taken a stab at me!* The procedure was officially called an "endoscopy." But I dubbed it "Operation Deep Throat," or "ODT" for short.

The doctor told me not to worry about the upcoming procedure. "We do this all the time. You won't remember a thing. *Yeah, right.* "You'll be placed into twilight state, and the lighted tube we insert down your throat is very small. You'll hardly know it's there." I then learned from the doctor that not only was I supposed to be semi-awake during ODT, I was supposed to assist him by swallowing the tube—on command.

When I agreed to ODT, I was all for being a cooperative patient, provided that I would be completely comatose. Now I worried about the procedure and sure as hell didn't know how I was going to scream, "You people took a wrong turn at my liver," while gagging on the tube. Of course, Kim insisted the procedure was utterly ridiculous and unnecessary, because the only thing they were going to find was a possessed fetus waving back at them.

Before the doctor scheduled the date for the ODT, he gave me a sonogram. Normally this is no biggie, but try keeping a gallon of water "down" and "in" without springing a leak somewhere while your stomach and bladder are being squished. It was a tall order even for me, the most seasoned patient.

"Have you had a pregnancy test yet?" he inquired, daring

me to pee on his table as he continued with his sonogram wand, spreading the warm jelly across my stomach.

"Oh, please!" I replied. "I am not pregnant. I can't get pregnant. I have endometriosis. I wish people would quit asking that," I blurted as I tried not to trickle. After three years of trying to conceive, the topic of pregnancy wasn't one I handled well.

On the day of ODT, I was asked four more times if I wanted a pregnancy test. I declined—all four times—demanding my "happy shot" instead to put me into twilight sleep.

When I was rolled to the operating room, I was still coherent enough to spot the day-spa torture chamber that awaited me. There were the usual IV catheters, several large syringes, a TV monitor, and an assortment of various large rubber tubes that dangled from the wall like giant octopus arms.

For days, I was on pins and needles awaiting my results. I was making out my will when the nurse called and requested that I come to the office immediately to speak to the doctor.

"Oh, quit your whining and take a blood test already," Kim said impatiently when I called her, crying about the ominous call from the nurse. "I've already bought you a case of Pampers for when you're ready to admit the obvious."

My mother went with me to the doctor's office. Finally, my name was called and the two of us followed the nurse into an exam room. By the time the doctor came in, I had worked myself into a frenzied terror.

"Is it my pancreas? Is it cancer?" I blurted, as the doctor stood stone-faced, looking at my chart. He handed me the photo from my sonogram and I nearly passed out when I saw the size of the growth inside my stomach.

"Oh, God! How long do I have?" I asked, as Mama took my hand. Both of us were now crying.

"About six more months," he said. "Maybe a little less."

Six months! I nearly fainted, as did Mama, before he added, "This is the first time I've ever had to tell one of my patients she is pregnant."

"Pregnant? Me? You mean I don't have stomach cancer or even a mild case of botulism?" I asked, in total disbelief.

Yes, I was pregnant. In the blink of an eye, I went from worrying about wearing my hair up or down at my own funeral to learning I would become a mother in just six months. Never mind the whopping $700 we inadvertently spent on medical procedures to find out that the rabbit was, indeed, dead. That was one expensive pregnancy test. Poor rabbit.

Gestation Citations

by
Melissa Face

Most pregnant women have met them, perhaps even been stopped by them. And a ticket? Well, that's not out of the question either. Anything is possible when you encounter the pregnancy police.

I first met these constables of conception when I announced my pregnancy to co-workers. People who had barely muttered "good morning" to me in the past were suddenly concerned about whether I had signed up for a short-term disability policy or wondered if I had a flexible spending account for the baby's medical care. I assured them that I had everything under control. In reality, I had just gotten used to the idea that a baby was actually inside me. Though they meant well, the pregnancy police managed to make me feel more inadequate than I ever could have imagined.

As my baby grew, so did the list of suggestions from the

pregnancy patrol. I was issued a warning for coffee drinking in the break room at work. "You really should switch to decaf," a concerned citizen offered. "Caffeine is not good for the baby. And remember that brownies contain caffeine, too." I thanked her for the reminder and went on with my business.

A few weeks later, I came down with a terrible sinus infection and missed work for two days. When I returned, I was swiftly subpoenaed to my department's meeting area. A panel of investigators wanted to know what was wrong.

"Have you had a fever?"

"How high was it?"

"You know you can only take Tylenol, don't you?"

I did know. But I thanked them for their concern and returned to my desk.

Tired, nauseous and congested, I did my best to fly beneath the radar of the pregnancy police. I walked quickly in the hallways, hid behind piles of work on my desk and avoided the break room. But they always discovered me, even if to simply point out that I was "starting to show" and would soon need to shop for maternity clothes. I really appreciated their observations, especially the ones about my increasing chest size.

My co-workers weren't the only undercover officers I ran into. Oh, no—the pregnancy police often were plain-clothed neighbors, churchgoers and friends. They could spot a pregnancy "glow" from across town, and they were eager to pat a protruding belly in the cereal aisle of the grocery store.

I sometimes met up with them at 7-Eleven's Slurpee counter. "Don't have too many of these, now. You don't want to end up with gestational diabetes." No, I sure didn't. I quickly reached for a smaller cup and went to the cashier to pay.

The pregnancy police weren't trying to scare me—they were merely providing a public service. After all, it was their duty to warn me of the harmful effects of caffeine and the risks of gestational diabetes and off-limits medications. And they didn't mean to annoy me when they rattled off their lists of "You shoulds."

"You should consider breast-feeding."

"You should start looking for a pediatrician."

"You should sign up for a birthing class."

"How far along are you? Twenty weeks? You should be feeling some movement by now." But I hadn't, and their suppositions were making me even more nervous.

Recently, I met two girlfriends for lunch. We hadn't seen each other for ages.

"You're really five months?" one questioned me. "Good grief! You hardly even look pregnant!" I knew she meant well, but her remark made me wonder if my baby was developing properly. Suddenly, I couldn't wait for my next obstetric appointment.

For the majority of our meal, my friends' badges remained hidden. We caught up on the statuses of high-school classmates, gossiped about people in town and laughed over stories from our teenage years.

But every once in a while, I would catch a knowing look in response to something I said about my pregnancy or plans for motherhood. I stopped talking and smiled, realizing I was under surveillance. My friends asked me how many children

I planned to have. "Three," I responded, confidently. One winked at the other from across the table. It was a gesture that said, "Let's wait and see how she feels after this first one."

Although sometimes annoying and occasionally intrusive, these comments come from people who truly care. My co-workers, friends and neighbors just wish to share their experiences and impart their wisdom.

These women have knowledge that comes only from having conceived, delivered and raised their own babies. I am a child-rearing novice and thus grateful for their advice, warnings and suggestions. After all, it takes a village to raise a child, perhaps even to bring one to full term. And every village needs a police force.

Tyson, Melissa and Evan

The Innies and Outies of Motherhood

by
Suzanne Olsen

When they announced that I had a healthy 9-pound 5-ounce redheaded baby girl, the first thing I thought was, *Where does her red hair come from?*

Quite frankly, I was shocked and worried. Don't get me wrong—I was happy that my baby was healthy and robust, as evidenced by her yowling the whole time the nurses were cleaning and weighing her. What worried me was the red hair. In those first moments of my baby's life, I flashed back to my childhood friend growing up and her frizzy red hair. I remembered kids saying things like, "I'd rather be dead than red on the head."

I learned quickly that what I should have been worried about was the reputation redheads have for bad tempers. One particular fit of crying led to a frantic call to the pediatrician and years of covering my daughter's tummy to hide her . . . well, I'm getting ahead of myself.

She was an easy baby—slept well, didn't fuss, smiled a lot—but even as a tiny infant, if there was something she didn't like, her red-faced bawling let us know instantly.

Unfortunately, the thing she despised most in the world was getting her diaper changed. Maybe it was the changing table or the cool air when the diaper came off. Maybe she just didn't like having to stop the important things she was doing, such as shaking a rattle or cooing at a sunbeam. Whatever it was, when that diaper came off, it was as if someone had turned on the "screaming" switch, and it didn't stop until I picked her up after the fresh diaper was in place.

One day, her diaper was packed full, and I knew I was in for an ear-shattering changing session. I got everything ready beforehand then worked as fast as I could. It was a particularly stinky, sticky mess, and I knew from experience that if I didn't get her cleaned thoroughly, she'd get a rash due to her fair skin.

I raised my voice above the howling and said happy things like, "Oh, don't we LOVE getting our diaper changed? Yes, we DO!" This only seemed to anger her more. Her mouth formed a giant "O" in a cherry-red face, her eyes squeezed shut and her fists balled up in the air and vibrated with anger. Her belly was taut, her toes pointed. All 25 inches of her four-month-old body raged in savage protest.

Then it happened. I was positioning the clean diaper when she arched her little back in a final wave of infant fury, and her belly button innie became an outie right before my eyes. It popped out like a Tender-Timer in a turkey and stuck out about an inch. I freaked out.

And she stopped crying. I don't know if she felt it pop or if she reacted to my astonished face and "holy crap!" exclamation. I finished changing the diaper in sheer panic and raced to call the pediatrician. The advice nurse listened to my breathless recounting of events and finally said, "It's OK. Nothing to be worried about. It won't hurt a thing."

"But what do I do?" I asked. "It's sticking OUT!"

"We can have her wear something around her waist to try to push it back in, but it will probably just pop back out again. Don't worry. She'll grow out of it."

"When?" I asked. I was truly concerned. Being a redhead *with* an outie would probably doom my poor sweet baby to decades of ridicule and abuse.

The nurse reassured me that it might take a few years, but the protruding belly button would go away. After I hung up, I cautiously touched the outie. It gave with my finger and felt like an air bubble inside a tied-off balloon. Each time I pushed it in, it popped back out like one of those Whac-A-Mole arcade games.

After that day, my baby never cried again while she had her diaper changed, so the outie became a good thing for my sanity. And for the record, the red hair became an asset for my daughter. People stopped us everywhere we went to ask about her beautiful hair, which was the color of a Golden Retriever with hints of copper.

Her belly button stuck out for years, but eventually it went back to normal. I made sure her little tops covered her middle, and I only bought her one-piece swimsuits. We all got used to it and never really noticed it after the initial shock.

As for the temper, it's still going strong. When my daughter doesn't like something, she goes from zero to 60 on the anger scale in about three seconds. One minute she's laughing and the next, she's running to her room and slamming the door so hard that pictures fall off the walls.

I can honestly say that learning the innies and outies of motherhood has been an eye-opening experience, especially with a redhead.

The redhead's outie

Second Time Around

by
Madeline McEwen

Wrong century or wrong continent? I couldn't figure it out. When I had a kid 20 years ago in England, being a mom was easy—I popped her out, packed her off to the child-minder and dashed back to work.

But when I became pregnant the second time, we were living in California. And something weird happened—this pregnancy would turn out to be a mind-bending experience.

It was like a dose of schizophrenia. How could I have gone from a full-time career woman to a full-time stay-at-home mom? That wasn't the plan. My Green Card was coming as was my bright new career. And there were many other things I hadn't calculated, like impending menopause and last chances. So instead of complaining, I shut up and knuckled down when I learned I was pregnant again. *Shouldn't this be easier the second time around?* I wondered. I wasn't sure, and, unfortunately, getting a Green Card takes far longer than growing a baby. With luck the baby would arrive months before the right to work ever did.

This time, I had several things going for me since we lived in Silicon Valley where first-time moms were a dime a dozen. If there's a huge gap between Baby #1 and Baby #2, the male powers-that-be treat an expectant mother like a virgin—well, almost. There is a special term for women who are at least 35 years old and pregnant for the first time—"elderly primagravida." Now if that doesn't make you want to apply for your pension, what does?

But I didn't officially fall into that category, even though I was 38. Things were different this time. So much had changed during the intervening years, and it wasn't just continental drift. Today's mom gets to make a plan about the birth of the baby. Instead of rushing to the hospital when her contractions are four minutes apart, the mother-to-be gets to choose when, where and how. Imagine that!

The first time around, I gave birth the way nature intended. The second time around, I had options. How about a water birth? Now that sounded fun, or if not exactly fun, at least a darn sight better than being shot full of drugs, upended like a turtle and having to push uphill.

I discussed the plan with my husband. If he had any opinions, I didn't give him a chance to tell me. This was my turn to be a diva, not that he had ever expressed any diva intentions himself.

Plowing through magazines, I marveled at the possibilities: candles, mood music, fluffy socks. I'd be free to wander around the hospital at will, whenever I wanted—pausing, panting, squatting. It sounded too good to be true. I couldn't believe that so much had changed in only 20 years. All those moms lucky enough to be pregnant in the 21st century received the gold-plated birth package. God bless America and its liberated womenfolk!

Although I had wanted a woman for my OBGYN, sadly, her appointment book was full. Never mind—my guy, Dr. Brown, was the real deal. Hadn't he already helped thousands of other women give birth? I decided it was better to have a seasoned traveler than a fresh-faced female.

My due date was determined, and I started counting down the days. Although I didn't bloom, I certainly grew, or rather my belly did. But although I felt like a whale, Dr. Brown wasn't quite so sure. He decided to assess the size of the fetus. I was alarmed. I didn't know much about medical procedures, but an X-ray seemed like a bad idea to me. How could he assess my baby while it was still inside me? I visualized Dr. Brown and his team whipping the baby outside on an elastic placenta for a quick weight and measurement before snapping it back inside me again. The thought gave me nightmares. But I needn't have worried. Instead, an ultrasound told the doctor all he needed to know.

"I'm sorry to tell you," he said to both my husband and me, "but your baby is not progressing as we would wish."

Although his words penetrated my brain, unfortunately everything else he said washed over me like mud. The men— my husband and the doctor—continued to talk, but their conversation might as well have been in Swahili.

We left the room, my husband in a state of stoic command,

but I felt like a slightly squashed jellyfish with tangled tendrils and sharp electric pangs in my brain.

Later, when we arrived home, my husband explained.

"It's really quite simple," he said. "If the baby doesn't grow enough, you'll be induced on the 15th of December. So no water birth, I'm afraid. And the candles are snuffed."

"Induced?" I squeaked. "You mean, drugged?"

"It's only the drug that your body already produces to tell the baby when to vacate the premises."

I vaguely recall a heated argument with lots of screaming. I think I was the screamer.

A tiny shred of hope percolated through the back of my mind. If a woman's first baby is early, it is highly likely that her second baby will also be early, like mine was. I clung to that remnant and prayed that this baby would appear on any day, or night, prior to the 15th of December.

Come the 13th of December, I was an active mommy-to-be. Everyone knows that strenuous physical activity can sometimes prod a lazy baby to perk up and pop out. When that didn't work, I tried eating curry in the evening. Everyone knows that spicy foods can sometimes speed up nature.

The next day, after a strenuous night with my husband (another known remedy), I plunged myself into the hottest bath feasible without risking third-degree burns. The belly bump sat above the waterline, irresolute, rigid and showing no hint of interest.

By midday, I grew more inventive, more desperate and more determined. I had concocted a whole list of ingredients that were supposed to speed things along—lemons, evening primrose, castor oil—

but cocktails of any flavor seemed unappetizing.

My husband appeared at the other side of the kitchen counter. He had spent the entire morning decorating the house for the holidays while I was occupied with calisthenics and timers. Usually oblivious to anything barring an earthquake, he put his firm hand on my fat-fingered one, which no longer wore a wedding band since it didn't fit anymore.

"You've nothing to worry about," he said, although even to my pulsating, blood-engorged, high-pressured ears, he didn't sound convincing. "This time tomorrow, it'll all be over." I didn't want to challenge him. *I might still be in labor by then,* I thought. But I also had another thought, a better thought—the birth would be over, and the rest of the baby's life would just be beginning.

I slept better than I thought possible that night.

The next day, while we were heading to the hospital, I suddenly wondered what I'd been worried about. This might not have been the original plan, but it was still better than a stable.

Although we had had a tour of the hospital facility some months back, I was surprised by how much it resembled a fancy hotel: chintz floral curtains, tiebacks, thick carpet on the perimeter. The room was airy and spacious—enough for a complete maternity team of experts with plenty of elbowroom.

I tried not to listen to the woman screaming in the next room. Instead, I focused on distracting myself from needles and metal paraphernalia. Still, I had hours and hours to worry, from eight in the morning until four that afternoon. I'm not sure exactly what I expected. It wasn't as if the drugs would enter my system and the the baby would obligingly appear with the next breath, but as luck would have it, she did eventually make an appearance.

Dr. Brown stood in position. He put me in mind of some famous sports personality, although I'm not sure which one. Dr. Brown wore an expression of great concentration, as if any minute he would be called upon to perform some great feat of daring-do. And he did. When my daughter shot across the room like a slick cannonball, Dr. Brown caught her like a professional fielder without even breaking a sweat.

If ever there were a time to be grateful to the great god of sport, this was the exact second. And for now, at least, it was the right century, and definitely the right continent.

Cutting Corners

by
Elizabeth Philip

Forget stranger danger. It was daddy danger that frightened me. As a soon-to-be mother, I spent months before our son's birth scouring parenting magazines for articles detailing the safest sleeping positions, rating car seat and highchair safety and outlining potential food dangers. Vigilant by nature, I implored my husband, Mitch, to join my crusade to ferret out hidden risks, but he showed little interest. I dog-eared magazine articles and displayed the publications on the dining room table, the bathroom counter and his office desk hoping to garner his attention.

"Have you read the article on tethering the television stand to the wall?" I asked.

He waved off my concern. "Our parents didn't worry about every possible accident that could happen, and we lived right through it."

"Maybe our parents didn't care about us," I suggested.

He laughed. "Our parents were sensible. The Chicken Little people just want to sell you products that we don't need."

But I continued to believe the world was a dangerous place.

The next day, when we were both in the kitchen, Mitch noticed the altered pull cord on the miniblinds above the sink. "What happened?" he asked.

"Oh, I cut them all."

He looked around the room at the other sliced pull cords. "Any particular reason?"

Annoyed by his lack of knowledge, I said, "Because they can kill. That's why." I walked over, put my head between the cords as if they were still intact and feigned a hanging episode. "See, a toddler could choke himself."

Mitch watched, unimpressed. "Yeah, if he were 6 feet tall and washing the dishes."

"That's not the point," I said.

"What exactly *is* the point?"

I sighed, frustrated that he didn't understand my worries.

"Besides," he added, "guys don't volunteer to wash dishes, and we're having a boy."

He had a point. I admitted I was jittery, unsettled about this new-mother thing, and that, perhaps, hypervigilance had hijacked my common sense. I suspected that my addiction to creating a baby-friendly environment would ease once Ellis arrived, and I would realize parenthood wasn't so scary after all.

But after his birth, my anxiety only heightened, and I continued my mission of safeguarding by scoping the aisles at Babies"R"Us each month in search of new products. They had locks and latches for everything, which Mitch soon realized as he tried unsuccessfully to open the oven and pantry doors. Next came the kitchen and bathroom cabinet locks, the anti-scalding device for the tubs, the electrical outlet covers and bumper pads for the living room tables. We would need baby monitors on every level of the house, as well as gates and doorknob covers. *How did I ever survive my childhood?* I wondered.

Mitch stood in front of the door leading to the garage, attempting to leave for work, the knob cover spinning around and around as he turned it without success. "For Pete's sake. Can't a man leave for work?"

I pushed him aside. "No offense," I said, "but everything's been childproofed." I pinched the cover together, turned the knob with ease, opened the door and smiled.

He grabbed his briefcase and turned toward me. "How many more months of this?"

"The day Ellis leaves for college, we should be good."

That was if our son lived that long. It was one thing for Mitch to refuse to embrace my safety precautions, but another when he became a one-man safety hazard. Arriving home one day, I found Ellis in his bouncy seat atop the kitchen island, inches from the edge. Still bouncing. Alone.

I grabbed the seat from the counter and placed it on the floor, my hands shaking. "Mitch!" I called.

He came down the staircase. "Oh, you're back early."

"And thank God. How could you leave Ellis in the bouncy seat on the kitchen island while you're out of the room? He could've flung himself over the edge and died."

"But he didn't. And, for your information, I put him up off the floor so the dog wouldn't get to him. But do I get any credit for that? No."

"Are you serious?"

"Didn't you read the article about babies and dog bites?" He held up the magazine on the kitchen counter.

He read a parenting magazine? I needed to reward the behavior, so I went easy on him. "Next time, take him upstairs with you. OK?" That idea would be short-lived since, once Ellis was a toddler, there'd be new dangers—the staircase, the bathtub and the toilet.

As Ellis grew, so did my anxiety. Soon, I was no longer the sole provider of Ellis's nutrition. His father also fed him. And the consumption of solid foods brought a new fear of impending death by choking.

It was time for a talk with Daddy. Whipping out an empty toilet paper roll, I wiggled it in the air.

"I know. I know," Mitch said. "I should've changed the roll. My bad."

"Who cares about that? We have much bigger concerns." I held the roll in front of me. "Anything that can fit through this hole is a choking hazard to a toddler." To demonstrate, I took a small super ball toy and dropped it through the roll. The ball bounced across the kitchen tiles, and the dog swooped in and caught the ball in his mouth.

Mitch laughed. "And if Caesar chokes?"

"Crap," I said, as I leaned over and pried the ball from Caesar's mouth.

"Now, before you hand any food or toys to Ellis, I want you to perform the toilet-paper-roll test."

"You're kidding, right?"

"No. And, as far as food goes, don't give him any grapes, popcorn, hot dog chunks, globs of peanut butter and bread or . . ."

"Wait. Isn't he only getting breast milk right now?"

"Yeah."

He grabbed the empty paper roll and peered through it at my chest. "Using this standard of measurement, your breast barely passes the test."

"Very funny." I snatched the roll back. "When you're ready to be serious, let me know."

A couple of weeks later, I came home from the grocery store to find Mitch standing in the kitchen, making a sandwich. I glanced around the room. "Where's Ellis?" I asked.

"Oh," he said, "he's in the La-Z-Boy recliner."

"What?"

"He's in the La-Z-Boy. I thought he might want to sit up for a while."

"He's not old enough to sit up!" I tossed the bag of groceries on the countertop and rushed to the living room to find our three-month-old son toppled on his side like a cow in a field tipped over by bored teenagers. I lifted Ellis into my arms and cradled him. Then I marched back to the kitchen. "What were you thinking, propping him up in the chair like that? He doesn't have the neck muscles to hold up his head yet. He could've fallen over and suffocated himself."

"Or he could've just enjoyed an afternoon nap in front of

the TV like millions of men all across America."

To Mitch, the La-Z-Boy incident was a rite of passage. To me, it was a gross oversight that could have maimed our son. Soon we became entrenched in our different styles of parenting and chanted our mantras whenever we disagreed.

"You can't ever be too safe," I said repeatedly.

"Don't make him a momma's boy," Mitch warned. "The kids will beat him up at school."

Beat him up at school? Geez, I hadn't even thought of that yet.

Throughout the coming months, each new milestone brought new safety concerns. When Ellis started crawling, dog hair became a food group that I was forced to accept. His walking turned our house into a gated community, and the hiking of legs up and over the gates by Mitch and me led to pulled groin muscles. I had to remind Mitch that it was a small price to pay for Ellis's welfare.

Four years later, our daughter Ava was born, and I no longer had time to shower, yet alone read parenting magazines. Out of necessity, Ellis had to become more independent. While nursing Ava, Ellis held up a yogurt cup and asked me, "Mommy, can I have a spoon?"

"You can get it yourself from the kitchen. You know a spoon from a knife, right?"

He nodded. I listened as he foraged in the silverware drawer. Then there was prolonged silence. *No screaming, no worries,* I thought.

Silence from the room in which Ellis played no longer frightened me. Rather, I welcomed the break from the hundreds of daily requests that exhausted me as I tried to balance Ava's needs with Ellis's wants. I no longer viewed the house as a deathtrap, but instead, as Ellis's bountiful playground, so off went the locks, the latches and the knob covers.

One day, Mitch arrived home from work early and stood in the nursery doorway while I changed Ava's diaper. "Why is Ellis cutting the dog's hair?"

I looked over my shoulder and shrugged. "Do you have time to take the dog to the groomer?" I asked.

"Good point."

The Accidental Kidnapper

by
Catherine Giordano

I had to wait nine months for my child to arrive, just as most mothers do. However, there was one big difference. It wasn't nine months of gestation. It was nine months of dealing with the adoption rigamarole. Finally, my husband and I were able to go to Guatemala to finalize the adoption and bring our son home to New Jersey.

And, like most mothers, I held my child in my arms to celebrate his birth and his addition to the family. But I didn't hold him on the day he was born; the first time I held him was five years later, on his fifth birthday.

His Guatemalan birth certificate listed him as Juan Diego. I decided his new American birth certificate would list him as John David. This way, I would not totally change his name, but would Americanize it. For the first few months after the adoption, I called him "John Juan" until he got used to his new name.

John was now my son. I was now his mother. Little did I know that John did not immediately think of me as his mother—he thought of me as his kidnapper. I didn't understand this until about two years later.

One morning, as we ate breakfast in our kitchen, John told me about a dream he had the night before. "I was at an airport," he said. "Kidnappers brought me to the airport, but I escaped. I told the lady who sells the tickets, and she called the police."

I was just about to tell him, "Very good, that is exactly what you should do in a situation like that." I had given him the stranger-danger talk only a week earlier, so I thought that had prompted the dream. I had put off talking to him about this because I hated to destroy his innocence. I hated having to tell him he couldn't trust people and that there were some people who wanted to hurt children.

But before I could speak, he continued. "The kidnappers were you and Daddy," he said. "The police came and took the kidnappers away, and then they took me home to you, and we were so happy to see each other again." So, in his dream I was both the kidnapper and the person who represented home and safety. He apparently did not see any contradiction in that.

And that is how I realized I was a kidnapper, albeit an accidental kidnapper.

I should have understood a lot sooner. Although John learned English quickly and seemed to be a happy child, there were some clues.

For the first three months, he would not call me, "Mom."

He called me, "Hey, You." I didn't make an issue of this, and eventually, he started calling me "Mom" on his own.

There was also the incident with the security alarm in our home. John was standing next to me one morning when I went to turn the alarm off. "Looks like I forgot to turn on the alarm last night," I said more to myself than to John.

My son immediately became upset. "Mom!" he cried out, "How could you forget the alarm? Someone could have come in during the night and stolen me."

John's shyness around strangers could have been another clue. It didn't occur to me at the time, but perhaps he was shy because he was worried about being kidnapped. He might have been thinking, *I was kidnapped once—perhaps I'll be kidnapped again.*

I felt so happy about the adoption that I failed to see things from John's perspective. Consequently, I didn't think about how really tough adoption is on a five-year-old child, especially when he is adopted from another country. He had so much to cope with— new family, new house, new country, new climate, new language, new food, new school, new friends and even a new name.

I tended to focus on all the good things. In Guatemala, he used to sleep on the floor, but now he had his own bed with his own personal zoo of plush animals. In the morning, he'd come into my bed and we'd snuggle up to watch *Sesame Street* together before I took him to preschool. At night, I'd sit in an overstuffed chaise and he'd sit between my legs, nestled against my chest with a book on his lap, as I peered over his shoulder to read him a bedtime story.

He liked me to tell him the story about his adoption.

"Once upon a time," I would begin, "there was a little boy in Guatemala . . ." The story ended, "And then he got on a big airplane with his new mommy and daddy and flew to his new home, and everyone lived happily ever after."

Everything seemed fine to me. It did not occur to me that John felt like he had been kidnapped.

Fortunately, children are resilient. One day, not long after the kidnapping dream, I saw that John actually had good feelings about the adoption. I overheard him talking to his friend, telling him he was born in Guatemala. His friend said, "You are so lucky to be born in Guatemala!" Evidently this other boy was in awe that he knew someone who had been born in such an exotic place.

John vehemently disagreed. "No, I'm not," he said emphatically. "I was lucky to be adopted and come to the United States where I have a nice bed to sleep in, and a mom who doesn't hit me and good food to eat. In Guatemala, all we ever had was chicken-and-rice soup."

Apparently, sometimes getting kidnapped can be a good thing.

John in Guatemala

One and the Same

by
Barbara Carpenter

In the 1960s, amphetamines were legal. During that time, my second child arrived; and following his birth, I retained quite a few unwanted pounds on my 5 foot 4 inch frame.

At the baby's six-week checkup, I complained to the doctor that I really wanted to lose 40 pounds. He rummaged through his sample chest and handed me a small plastic box that contained 30 yellow-and-purple capsules. "Take one of these every morning before breakfast," he told me.

It didn't take long for me to fall in love. Now I had another little best friend in addition to my new baby. I popped a capsule into my mouth as soon as I got up and for the rest of the day, energy glowed inside my body like a constant, internal sunrise.

I had plenty of energy for my two-year-old daughter and new son . . . feedings, diaper changes, laundry, playtime and photos in assorted poses and outfits. Other new mothers complained about feeling frazzled, but not I! Before my son was a year old, I had lost nearly 50 pounds and could still run circles around the other young mothers. My doctor had no problem supplying me with these wonderful capsules, so life continued to be good.

When my son turned one, I decided I could do fine on my own, so I stopped taking the pills. Whoa! I could not get enough sleep. I napped when my kids did. At times, I felt as if I were walking through water—aware, but barely. My golden energy had disappeared.

That's when I wondered how any mother could keep up with so many demands. Within a month, I had gained five pounds, but not from overeating. On the pills, I could eat a normal diet, and continued to do so when I went off them.

Unfortunately, my doctor wouldn't give me any more of the happy pills. I complained to friends, all of whom were in their weight-conscious 20s. One of them had an answer.

"Go to Dr. Blank," she said. "You can walk into his office and tell the nurse you want some diet pills, and she'll give them to you." I didn't believe her, but I decided to give it a try. I had to find a way to keep up with my babies!

And it worked. The receptionist didn't even ask my name. For the next six years, I remained a svelte size 8, back when it really was a size 8! Periodically, I took breaks from the pills, but I found myself always going back to them.

During this time, I would occasionally hire a baby sitter so I could take short day trips with my husband. One late-winter day, I went with him to visit one of his suppliers, a man I had not met. I wore pink denim jeans and a pink pullover sweater, and I had styled my long blondish hair into a loose French twist. A little eye makeup completed my toilette.

The early March day proved to be practically balmy. I left my coat in the truck and took a stroll around the grounds. While my husband completed his business, I wandered among the veneer logs laid out in the log yard, sometimes stepping onto one so I could get a better view of the whole place, which was quite impressive. I could see the two men as they conversed in front of the large plate-glass window. They both waved to me when I turned toward them.

On the way home, my husband grinned at me. "You made quite an impression on the head honcho," he told me. "He thinks you are really cute—actually he said that you are beautiful."

I winked at him. "I am," I said. He chuckled.

"Modest, too, aren't you?" He touched my cheek. It was a good day.

Fast forward eight years. My children were no longer babies. They were in junior high, and I wore numerous hats: taxi driver, cook, laundress, maid, housekeeper, mother, wife/lover, referee and I even managed to maintain a small reupholstering business that kept me busier than I wanted to be. I was booked a year ahead, which sometimes made me feel trapped.

Did I forget to mention that the FDA had pulled the plug on my colorful diet pills? Well, anyone who has ever used amphetamines knows of their magic powers. I once heard someone say that it was easy to spot a woman who took them. She would be the one who, after a full day's work, would be outdoors sweeping her driveway with a whiskbroom at 3 A.M.

That pretty well described me during the pill years.

Of course, several of those lost pounds that I first started losing when my second child was born found their way home—home being my arms, legs, chins, hips, tummy, knees and whatever other parts of the body can be named. The total gain amounted to nearly 40 pounds! I constantly battled my excess weight, but not whole-heartedly. My hair had darkened with the years, and most workdays I didn't spend much, if any, time on it or makeup. After all, I was a stay-at-home mom who worked with dusty and sometimes dirty upholstered furniture. My job description did not include looking like a model.

My husband's business grew, and he crossed paths again with the buyer who had been so complimentary to me. One afternoon, that man came to our house, looking for my husband. He seemed surprised when I answered the doorbell.

"Oh, I'm sorry. I'm looking for the Carpenter residence."

"You've found it," I told him. "My husband will be here shortly. Would you like to come inside?"

"Oh, no, thank you. I'll wait in the car." I shrugged and closed the door after him.

That evening, my husband told me that the buyer thought he had remarried. "Get this, he said to me, 'The woman who opened the door isn't the cute little blonde you had up at my place a few years ago!' I told him it was, but he didn't believe me."

But my husband wasn't finished with the story: "Then, the guy's eyes got big, and he said, 'Wait a minute! Did you have a honey on the side? I didn't think you were that kind of guy! But I have to say that girl was a knock-out!'"

Story completed, my husband laughed. I didn't.

"You're making that up!" I accused.

"No, I'm not," he said. "He never did believe me that you were the same gal."

I didn't know whether to laugh, cry, hit him or kill the buyer. The positive thing that came from it was my decision to work seriously on the extra pounds.

Not long after the trauma, the same buyer came by again. My husband invited him in, and I served them coffee.

"By the way," I said, as I offered the man some homemade coffeecake. "I am the same woman you saw seven years ago at your log yard. I had just had two children and was on the right side of a diet that year. You now find me on the wrong side of one, but that's OK. You try having two babies and keeping your girlish figure—it's not easy. I'm happy with the way I feel and the way I look, and that's all that matters." I gave him a sweet smile, placed a full coffee pot on the table and exited.

The embarrassment on his face was worth every pound I had gained.

Call of the Wild

Terrible twos, troublesome threes . . .

Baby Book Bloopers

by
Terri Elders

In 1958 when my son Steve was born, nobody followed toddlers around with phone cameras, capturing their every action. Baby books and an occasional box-camera snapshot were the only ways to preserve important moments and events. I chronicled it all in my son's album: first smile, first tooth and first wave "bye bye."

And each time my growing-up-so-fast toddler uttered a new word—"toast," "car," "ball"—I faithfully dragged out his baby book and recorded it on the page titled, "Wonderful Words." My eyes then would stray to the adjacent page headed, "First Complete Sentence." I remembered my adoptive mother saying she'd heard that mine was, "See the moon."

I wondered what amazing observation Steve would soon make. My fingers already itched to capture his exact words. I anticipated the descriptive paragraph I'd compose, detailing the circumstances, the time, the place, the sights, sounds and smells. I wanted it to be something that he could look back on as an adult, something he'd be proud of and something he'd share one day with his own kids.

I knew from my own very recent experience that, as a teen, I blushed and rolled my eyes when Mama would recount my early years. But now that I'd reached young adulthood and had a little boy of my own, I'd prod her for more stories of my childhood every chance I could. I lamented that I'd had no baby book myself, since I'd been adopted at the age of five. I wanted to ensure that when Steve reached young adulthood, his own milestones would be at his fingertips and that he wouldn't feel bereft of a recorded past.

It took a minor leap of imagination to picture an adult Steve displaying his baby book to his wife or even his own grandchildren. "My mom was the best," he'd brag, I was certain. It was fun to give myself a mental pat on the back for being such a faithful scribe. He'd really appreciate this record of his early life.

Well into his second year, Steve started to gush and gurgle out new words daily. His vocabulary expanded so fast that I had to resort to scribbling all his words on the margins of that page labeled, "Wonderful Words." But when it came to actual sentences, I hesitated to record his first simple commands, those little grunts accompanied by gestures and pointing, the demanding, "Me go now" and "Want milk." I wanted more for posterity. Something with a more complex structure, something deeper, a little more literate. So I patiently waited for what I knew would be his true first perceptive commentary, something as profound as my first words, "See the moon." I didn't want my son shortchanged in the memory department.

When Steve was nearing two and a half, his dad and I took him on his first excursion to Marineland of the Pacific, a wonderful nearby oceanarium. I hovered over him, hoping for an utterance that I could at last classify as "First Complete Sentence." That page had remained blank far too long, and I was eager to tackle the next milestone.

Steve giggled at the antics of the dolphins, marveled at the seals and sea lions and gaped at Bubbles the Whale. But he mumbled no more than an occasional "funny" or "big."

As the afternoon drew to a close, we went into the gift shop. Even that nook was lined with miniature aquariums featuring strange and exotic sea creatures from all over the world, showcased in their natural environments.

As I debated whether I should purchase a shot glass embossed with the slogan, "A Whale of a Drink," or settle for a set of postcards featuring the so-called flying fish, Steve wandered a few feet over to stare at a baby octopus that had emerged from behind a chunk of coral. No more than 6 inches long, it unfurled its tentacles then drew them up tightly. Steve stared and stared as the denizen of the deep repeated its rhythmic movements.

A minute later, he shouted his first complete sentence, not merely an observation, but an actual inquiry. And everybody in the gift shop roared in appreciation. He nearly got a round of applause. But my cheeks flamed.

When we got home, I exchanged a rueful glance with my husband, and then went to the cupboard and dragged out the blue-bound book to write down Steve's blue-hued words. I recorded it all:

"Steve's first trip to Marineland; Saturday, August 16, 1960. Plenty of sunshine, sea breeze, scent of popcorn and cotton candy. And Steve's first words upon seeing a baby octopus: 'Mama, Daddy, what the hell is that?'"

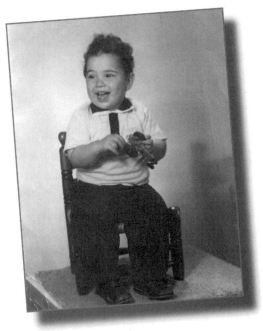

Steve, age 1

Tall Tales of Potty Training

by
Roselie Thoman

Listening to moms tell potty-training stories is a lot like listening to a collection of tall tales. You have to figure out where the truth stops and the larger-than-life storytelling begins.

Being new to the game—my first child, Cali, was ripe to start potty training—I believed their tales. My friends' kids were all potty trained in a day with hardly any effort at all. They were sporting big-kid underpants by 19 or 20 months, if not earlier. If, for some reason, they took more than a day to catch on, a shiny M&M would hook them.

I read the potty-training-preparedness section of my parenting book at least three dozen times in preparation for "P-Day." The book pointed out many things that I wondered about: *Can Cali undress herself?* She'd proved it the last time company was over when she undressed and ran around the living room. *Can Cali express herself verbally?* Last week, while out shopping for clothes, she shouted, "Look! Mommy boobies! Mommy boobies!" as we passed the bras. *Does Cali show an interest in the potty?* I don't remember the last time I had a private bathroom break to myself since she learned how to crawl.

With all signs checked off the list and Cali a month shy of her second birthday, her father and I brought home a new potty.

"Here you go!" we said, placing the potty in the bathroom. We stood back and waited with great anticipation as she sat down for the first time. Never had we been so excited about someone sitting on a potty.

After a couple of days of intermittent interest with no results, I bought a pack of M&M's. I wasn't sold on the idea, but I'd been assured by moms and grandmas that it was the secret to potty-training success. Still, it seemed there was something wrong with bribing a child with food to use the bathroom.

Cali didn't get candy very often, so when she saw the bright chocolate treats, her eyes lit up.

"If you put your pee-pee in the potty, you get one! If you put your poo-poo in the potty, you get two!"

Cali ran right to her potty, sat down and went pee-pee. We washed her hands, went to the kitchen and chose a yellow candy.

"Yummy!" she cried as she ran back down the hall to her potty, sat down and eked a bit more out.

I helped her wash her hands. We then went back to the kitchen and she chose a blue one.

"Yummy!" she cried and ran down the hall a third time, sat down and, with great determination, managed to produce one more teeny, tiny drop. She washed her hands then held them out for a third M&M.

The combination of candy, over-the-top praise and the excitement of using the potty led to Cali running up and down the hall naked, cheerfully screaming at the top of her lungs, while my husband, who worked nights, was trying to sleep.

"Mini M&M's! The mini ones!" a friend advised when I told her about that endless afternoon. I returned to the store and bought a tube of the little ones.

Cali was not impressed. "I want BIG ones!"

After days went by and she still wasn't fully potty trained, I sought more advice.

"Let her run around naked," I was told. It wasn't warm enough to be outside in the buff, so Cali ran around naked in our living room. After several accidents on our new carpet, my husband covered the entire living area with a blue tarp. Three days later, with no further progress, we gave up on that idea.

"Just take the diapers away." Out went the diapers and on went the training panties. After a few days of consistently using the training pants as if they were diapers, and me throwing out three pairs of poo-filled ones, the diapers came back.

"A sticker chart!" I went online, downloaded a chart and placed it on the fridge. I dug out a pile of stickers. Cali liked stickers, but did not like the idea of putting them on a paper instead of on her hand, leg or face. She liked the stickers, but not enough for all the trouble it was to use the potty.

"Prizes!" Desperation kicked in. We'd been doing this for

months now with little progress. She'd use the potty when she felt like it, but if she was busy or not in the mood, she didn't. I went to the dollar store, filled my basket with toys and made a treasure box. She was so excited! But after the treasure box was empty, the incentive to use the potty was over. I refilled the treasure chest and, once again, when the treasure was gone, using the potty stopped. My budget called it quits on that plan.

"They'll be ready when they're ready." Away went the panties. Away went the prizes. Away went the stickers. Back were the diapers. Cali was happy as a clam.

We switched to Pull-Ups and watched *Elmo's Potty Time* more than 100 times. Eventually, Cali started using the potty on her own without incentive . . . except for when it came to Number Two.

"Oh Mommmyyy, I made a surprise for yooouuu!" was the greeting I'd get after nap time.

Cali's third birthday was about a month away. Gymnastics would be starting soon. I wanted her to wear underpants under her leotard instead of a bulky Pull-Up. Plus, Pull-Ups weren't cheap!

After being low key and low pressure on the subject for many, many weeks, it was time to pull out all the stops. We had a "bye-bye diaper" celebration. The grandparents were invited, a cake was ordered and big-girl underpants were purchased and wrapped. We talked it up for days and had a countdown to underpants.

When the day arrived, we brought out the cake and sang our song to the tune of Happy Birthday—"No more diapers for you, no more diapers for you! You are such a big girl; no more diapers for you!" Everyone cheered.

Cali opened her presents. We went into her room and gathered up every last diaper and Pull-Up and moved them to her baby brother's room.

After that, we were just fine.

Now I have friends ask me about potty training. I'm sure they are hoping that when I tell them I tried everything, and it took a year, I am merely sharing a tall tale.

Cali

The End of Mama

by
Candace Carrabus

Hard as I tried to prevent it, my three-and-a-half-year-old daughter learned about the dreaded Barbie doll via preschool.

OK, I know I'm not the only one repulsed by the thing, and not just because I didn't have one when I was a kid and all my friends did. I distrust this toy for her culpability in teaching our daughters to objectify themselves, not to mention her incredible proportions. Plus, anything surrounded by hype is suspect in my book. If Barbie, in all her incarnations and spin-offs, doesn't epitomize hype, nothing does.

My little darling wanted to know if she could have a Barbie. I said no at first, but resigned myself to the fact that eventually we'd end up with at least one version of the vile doll under our roof. So I decided to be proactive. If Barbie had to darken my door, I would control how and when. In the spirit of Michael Corleone's philosophy (or was it Sun Tzu?)—"Keep your friends close, but your enemies closer"—I bought one and hid it under my bed. And waited for the right moment.

An opportunity presented itself as an important upcoming passage loomed large on our horizon. The end of "mama." The end of breast-feeding my one-and-only child. Yes, even at age three, each morning my darling girl climbed into "the big bed" with us and indulged in a little "mama." I didn't want to wean her, and she wasn't too keen on the idea, either. The end of "mama" would be a big transition for us both.

We talked about celebrating in a way we'd both remember. I chose the day and tried to explain why she couldn't nurse until she went to college. Frankly, I had trouble coming up with a good reason for that and resorted to the tried-and-true, "You just can't." I'd like to say I thought of an appropriate ritual to mark the event, but nothing came to mind. Instead, I let her pick out a couple of new toys. This, I told myself, would make it easier for her, but it was really to relieve my own confused feelings.

At the store, my girl chose statues of a horse and foal I thought perfect, plus we purchased a "big-girl" nightgown. Princess-of-Ireland Barbie still waited under the bed to make her debut. I'd selected this model precisely because she didn't look like a typical Barbie doll. She had wavy red hair and green eyes. Of course, from her ridiculously long neck to her absurdly pointed toes, she was Barbie through and through.

When I suggested the Barbie I had at home also be part of our celebration, my daughter enthusiastically agreed. But while we wended our way through Walmart's aisles, she sat contentedly in the shopping-cart seat, keeping tight hold of the big box with the horses in it, staring through the clear plastic top at the paint mare and her colt.

In the checkout line, a young woman smiled and asked, "Do you have a new horsey there?"

"Yes!" my darling proclaimed loudly. "It's to celebrate the end of mama!"

The woman's gaze flicked over me as if she were speculating about the potential reason for my demise and why it was cause for celebration. I groaned inwardly. Suddenly, something perfectly natural sounded sinister. Of course, I felt the need to explain extended nursing and our desire to commemorate its conclusion. My sputtering over the euphemistic "mama" and how the word was a stand-in for both breasts and breast-feeding only garnered a more skeptical look. The woman, not too subtly, edged away. You'd think I'd announced we were going to sacrifice kittens at dawn.

After we had arrived home, we freed the horses from their cardboard and plastic corral, and I brought out Princess-of-Ireland Barbie. My daughter's face lit up as she took the package. She hugged and thanked me and held the box to her heart. I felt small and mean-spirited for wanting to deny her this pleasure. Surely, I could counteract the influence of one Barbie. I didn't have to like it, but maybe one wouldn't permanently corrupt my child. Still, I insisted we wait until the next day to unleash the thing.

That evening, the darling child donned her big-girl nightgown, and to my eyes looked nearly ready to go off to college. *Could it really be time for this so soon?* I thought. The new horses watched over her from the bedside table, and she stationed Princess-of-Ireland Barbie, still boxed, in the hallway between our bedrooms.

"To guard us," she said.

In many previous conversations, I'd stressed the importance that princesses—even Barbie princesses—be capable, kind and smart in addition to pretty. After a short discussion, we concluded the red-haired doll must possess these qualities. After all, how else could she be a princess? That's why she received the honored guard post.

Point for my side.

My girl-woman marched off to bed knowing the next morning would be the last time she would breast-feed. She was focused on getting Barbie when we were done, not consciously acknowledging she would never nurse again. Weeping about that was my job.

At daybreak, she asked for a little "mama," as she did every day. I was wistful. She was eager to play with her new doll. Reluctantly, I let her go, trying hard to be the grown-up of the two of us, knowing this to be only the first of many such separations that would be harder on me than on her.

Two points for Barbie.

A little later, though, after undressing and redressing the object of her desire, trying the unusable shoes on a couple of other dolls, "just like Cinderella," then unsuccessfully striving to make Barbie's stiff limbs straddle a horse, my daughter proclaimed the Barbie princess was pretty, but useless—particularly her smooth "mamas."

"They don't work," she said.

Game to me.

The horses, along with the rest of an ever-expanding herd,

get played with every day. Princess-of-Ireland Barbie, in her brocade gown, velvet cloak, gold tiara and non-functioning "mamas," sits forsaken on a dresser—shoeless, friendless—a lonely reminder that perfection is boring.

I pretend not to gloat.

The Other Woman

by
Amanda Mushro

I knew it would happen eventually, but I wasn't prepared for it to happen so soon.

Of course, I knew I wouldn't be the only girl in his life forever. But, damn it, I should have kept him inside that day. I let my son out of my sight at my in-laws' house for two minutes and, in that time, he caught a glimpse of the home-wrecker neighbor girl.

She was adorable with her wild blond hair. The fact she was slightly older than him was intriguing. And she had a rebellious side—she never wore shoes and refused to wear a helmet. Apparently, my boy "had a type."

He has tons of friends who are girls, and I usually have to remind him not to play so roughly. "Girls don't like to wrestle." "Girls don't like dirt thrown on them." "Girls don't appreciate headlocks." But the silly grin plastered on his face when this girl crossed the yard told me she wasn't the typical playmate.

When the shoeless gal strolled up to my boy, I was not prepared for what would unfold before my eyes. At the very least, I hoped my son would hold off on this love-struck behavior until middle school when I could ignore it or hide in the kitchen drinking wine straight out of the bottle.

It started with my son laughing a little too loudly at her jokes, agreeing to play games he usually doesn't like to play and attempting to put on her brother's roller blades because she wanted him to skate with her. I had to pull him out of the roller blades before he fell and broke his neck.

After I had filled the water table for the third time, I banned my son from tipping it over again. But I was no match for the girl, who giggled and laughed when my son "Hulked out" on the table, tossing it to the side and spilling the contents down the deck. Her siren call was too powerful, and the water went soaring across my feet in defiance.

Now I see your game, sir, I thought. I vaguely remembered his father pulling the same stunts, but with a beer and a funnel. Different tools, same effect.

Then as if he was starring in his own version of *Jackass*, the boy grabbed his little red bike and started peddling it down a grassy hill. He yelled to get the girl's attention just before he intentionally crashed. His dramatic fall was followed by a roll down the rest of the hill, ending with him lying at the bottom for a while—long enough for her to come running to see if he was OK.

When she asked me, "Can he come play in my house?" I told her "NO!" a little too forcefully. It wasn't because I want to shelter my boy or that I have a strange obsession with my son (well, maybe a little), but because after watching his moves and seeing him work his game, I needed to save that kid from his own devices. Plus, it was dinnertime.

My son has plenty of years to have crushes, but dear Lord, I cannot handle it right now. I'm not sure I will ever be able to handle it. So until I am ready, the only wild-haired blonde he needs in his life is his mama. Wow! If that statement doesn't say this kid will need therapy, I don't know what does.

Amanda's son Aaron

A Hairy Situation

by
Donna Volkenannt

In my late 20s, I was living the American dream—married with two children, a house in the suburbs and two cars in the garage. The downside of that dream was that with so many bills and one child in parochial school, my husband's paycheck didn't leave much to buy extras.

Our son Erik was four and daughter Julie, seven, when I decided it was time to go back to work. My husband, Walt, agreed it was a great idea.

After submitting résumés and applications, I was hired as a secretary-stenographer at the local Army agency where I'd worked before getting married. Returning to a full-time job after years of being a stay-at-home mom meant more than finding a baby sitter—I also needed a complete wardrobe makeover. Bell-bottom jeans and casual tops wouldn't cut it in an office environment.

One fall afternoon while Julie was in school, I strapped Erik into his car seat then picked up my sister Kathleen and her toddler, Ryan. The four of us headed for a local shopping center to find me some new duds.

Kathleen pushed Ryan in a stroller while I held onto Erik's hand, and we searched for a few new outfits. As I combed racks of dresses, Erik darted away and scampered around the store, ducking under shelves and playing hide-and-seek.

I chased him down and said, "Stop running around. You'll get hurt."

He didn't seem impressed until I added, "Or a stranger might grab you."

His bright blue eyes grew wide. A frightened look crossed his face. He pleaded, "Can we leave now?"

Giving him a hug, I said, "As soon as I finish shopping. If you're good, we'll stop for ice cream on the way home." That put a smile on his face.

A few minutes later, I had an armful of clothes to try on. On the way to the dressing room, Erik wiggled away and bumped into a middle-aged woman whose inky black hair was streaked with white. When I grabbed him by the hand and apologized to the woman, I noticed a large hairy mole on her chin and a dark mustache above her lip.

She waved off my apology. "He's adorable. A little towhead."

Erik stared at her and made a face. When she reached down to pat his white-blond hair, he ran to my sister, who stood near the dressing room while her son slept peacefully in the stroller.

Embarrassed by Erik's behavior, I shrugged. "He's a little shy around strangers."

The woman nodded and returned to her shopping.

In the dressing room, I slid a navy-and-white pinstriped dress over my head and started buttoning it up when I heard Kathleen yell, "Get over here! Your mom will be out in a minute!"

When I came out of the dressing room, Kathleen had her arms wrapped firmly around my son.

Standing in front of a three-way mirror to get a full view of my outfit, I noticed the woman with the mole on her lip standing nearby, watching us.

"So, what do you think?" I asked Kathleen.

"Cute," she said, as she struggled to keep my son from squirming away. "You should get it."

After examining the price tag, I nodded and turned to try on another dress.

"Mommy," Erik said, extending his arms, "hold me."

I kissed his forehead. "Mommy's almost finished, honey."

I was almost to the dressing room when I heard his scream. When I turned around, he had his blond head buried in my sister's neck. I hurried over and rubbed his back. "What's wrong, sweetie?"

He pointed to the dark-haired woman. "That lady," he pointed. "Why does she have a mustache?"

I'm not sure whose face was more red—hers or mine.

"Sorry," I said to the woman's back as she hurried out of the store.

Holding Erik out like a smelly fish, my sister said, "He's all yours."

On the drive home, Kathleen and I promised that if we ever noticed stray facial hairs where they shouldn't be, we'd let each other know.

The day before starting my job, I inventoried my work attire. I had everything to start my career: dresses, blouses, skirts, slacks, shoes, purse and pantyhose. And there was one additional purchase I made to ensure I looked my best before returning to the workforce—a new pair of tweezers.

Donna with daughter
Julie and holding Erik

Amen, Shucks

by
Georgia Mellie Justad

"Shucks," rang the voice from the back of the van. It was my precious baby Jack, who'd miraculously managed to utter his first, full-fledged word beyond his usual pointing and grunting.

It should have been one for the books, one where I would proudly record said word, the time, place and my reaction to such a milestone, except he didn't say "shucks." He said the other S-word. You know the one.

My hubby, Todd, and I looked at each other. Surely he didn't say that. Not my baby that I'd spent a week birthing. My hopes were quickly dashed 20 minutes later when Todd suddenly hit a bump and Jack dropped his sippy cup.

"Shit," he mumbled.

There was no mistaking it that time.

"I wonder where he learned that word?" Todd whispered to me, performing his best shock-and-awe impersonation.

"Yeah, I wonder," I growled, my dagger-eyes piercing his clueless puppy-dog ones.

Todd had been a master of that word as long as I'd known him. But since Jack's birth, Todd saved the special word primarily for Sunday-afternoon football games and driving.

The timing couldn't have been worse. We were on our way to my mother's house for Christmas.

"I'll bet they'll be surprised at how well Jack has learned to express himself since the last time they saw him," I said, sarcastically.

"Maybe it was a one-time thing," offered Todd. "Let's not make a big deal about it, and we'll see what happens."

I could only hope. Before we left for our long trip, I had spent hours strategically packing the van to the roof with presents, toys and luggage, leaving just enough room for the three of us to breathe if we turned our heads straight up. It had been several months since Mama and Daddy had seen Jack, and I was eager to show him off. Jack was at that wonderful age where he was beginning to do some really impressive things, such as going through my underwear drawer and dragging out various pieces of lingerie to show to company, or hiding his full juice cup in the dryer. He was the only toddler I knew who had mastered the art of tie-dying at age two and a half. If only he would learn to speak. Thus, I learned two things that day in the car: not only does God answer prayers, but He also has a wicked sense of humor.

As we drove northward along the Florida turnpike to Georgia, Jack was already squirming. *One hour down and 11 to go*, I thought. I popped Jack's favorite CD—the ever popular, noose-crocheting and hang-yourself-silly *Alvin and the Chipmunks*

Christmas—into the car's CD player in hopes of calming him. I even sang along, which agitated Todd with every word I belted out. However, 10 minutes later, Todd's mood lifted. It's amazing how tossing a defenseless CD out the window of a fast-moving van can change a man's entire holiday demeanor.

Staring out the window where Alvin and the Chipmunks now lay amongst the cow chips, I looked up in time to see a huge semi moving on top of us.

"Look out!" I screamed.

"Ah, man, shhh . . ." Todd said. A pile of presents shifted, tumbling into his lap.

"Todd, you better not say it," I warned.

But, it was too late. Little Jack finished his profane sentence for him.

"Nice going!" I whispered to my husband.

That's when Todd insisted he rarely used that word and perhaps Jack had picked it up from someone else.

"Please! The last time I checked, that word had never been one of Mr. Rogers' words for the day!"

"I'm sorry, honey. But sometimes that word is the only one that fits when no other will do," he justified.

"Are you kidding? That's your excuse for contaminating our baby? You'll have to do better than that. If you think I'm mad, you better know now that Mama is going to have your head!"

I looked back at my beautiful blond, blue-eyed angel sitting sweetly in his car seat. I became a basket case as I tried to figure out how to fix this mess before we got to Mama's and how to cut Todd's tongue out without bloodying the floor mats.

"Maybe we can deprogram him before we get to your mama's,"

Todd said, as if Jack was a computer on the fritz at his office.

I had visions of Mama opening her holly-wreath-adorned door, dressed in her festive holiday attire. She would scoop up her only grandchild and hug him tightly, saying, "Gramma loves you." Jack, in turn, would respond sweetly with, "Ah, man, shit, Gramma." This would be followed by a *thud* as Mama collapsed in a heap onto the front porch, dropping our smut-talking toddler in the magnolia bushes. It was too horrible to imagine.

I knew I had to work a little Christmas magic of my own. With only eight hours left to go, I had to get cracking. This would be my first exorcism.

"The only way around this is to teach both of you a new word," I said. "And fast."

And so for the remaining 700 miles, it was, "Aw, shucks" this and "Aw, shucks" that. It reminded me of being on the set of an old G-rated John Wayne Western, with a little Hopalong Cassidy and Slim Pickens thrown in for good measure.

I was impressed with how well my two boys were coming along with the new phrase, except when Todd would add the occasional, "What the shuck?" as he fought his way northward in the bumper-to-bumper traffic.

When we were close to our destination, I was optimistic that my idea would work. Todd agreed. "I can't believe we pulled it off," he said, declaring it to be a Christmas miracle as we passed the Cedartown, Georgia, city-limit sign.

Mama's driveway looked like a used car lot—it appeared that everyone from town was there. When she appeared at the front door with her beehive piled to perfection, it made sense.

It looked like she'd brought half the salon with her straight from Irmalene's, all of them eager to see my potty-mouthed prodigal son.

All in attendance remarked that Jack was such a well-behaved child. I hated to disillusion them, especially during the holidays, and prayed he'd have nothing "colorful" to say to my former Sunday school teacher, who was among the guests. *As long as she doesn't start a sentence with, "Ah, man," we might have this licked.*

I finally pulled Mama aside and told her that Jack had uttered his first, bona fide word.

"That's wonderful," she beamed as if Jack had discovered penicillin.

She was just about to announce the "good news" to the entire room when I whispered what that auspicious word was. She did better than I thought, requiring only three smelling salts instead of four. Naturally, she knew where that word had come from.

"You'd better straighten up!" she said to son-in-law Todd in her first-grade school teacher voice.

Daddy and my sister Kim, who had learned of Jack's special phrase, found the entire ordeal hilarious.

"What a fine example you're setting as the godmother," I said to Kim. "And you, too, Daddy," I scolded.

The next night, we attended the Christmas Eve candlelight service at the First Methodist Church where I had been baptized many years ago. To be safe, I instructed everyone to be mindful of what they said in front of Jack before we headed into church. In other words, nobody could say anything that sounded like "Ah, man."

Once inside, we took our seats in the last pew. All around me were people I hadn't seen in years. As the organ began to play, I found myself praying that Jack wouldn't speak a word.

Near the front of the church sat my high school English teacher. In the choir loft was my beloved high school German teacher. They both smiled and nodded approvingly at little angelic Jack who was standing on the pew next to me, clutching his blue blankie in his adorable Rudolph the Reindeer attire. So far so good.

I was beginning to relax when Jack began scooting on his back down the pew. His squeaky sneakers competed with the organ as he head-butted his way toward my father.

"Oh my, he certainly is active," remarked a woman in front of me.

Just then, the minister commanded us to pray. A hushed tone fell over the congregation. The organ played softly in the background, accompanied by Jack and his Squeaky Shoe Band.

"Be still, pumpkin," I whispered to Jack as the preacher began the prayer.

Jack dropped to the floor, playing with his favorite Matchbox car at my feet. We opened our hymnals and began to sing. Suddenly, Jack was on the move, now underneath Mama's feet, happily making honking noises as he drove his car over her boots.

As the congregation sang out a hearty "A-men" at the end of the hymn, the room fell silent. *Amen,* I thought. *Oh, no! A-men!*

Jack suddenly popped up from the floor like a stripper

from a cake and belted out, "Shit!" at the top of his lungs. There were a few gasps from the choir loft, as well as down front near the pulpit where several prissy little old ladies sat, the preacher's mama included, all dressed in their Christmas fancy hats and corsages. I'm surprised none of them fainted. They were the type who'd stiffen if you dared sneeze in church.

I looked at Mama, whose face was the same color as her scarlet Christmas sweater, and not in a good way. Mama did look in Todd's direction, and, God help him—that one look said it was his fault and that I would be a widow before the service was over. Given the situation, I planned to help her.

One nanosecond later, explosions of laughter swept through the century-old sanctuary. Everyone joined in, including my family.

And as for me, I sat mortified, hiding behind my program. Todd was right. Sometimes it really is the only word that will do.

Jack (age 3) and dad, Todd

Pavlov's Dogs and Potty Training

by
Shari Courter

We started our family when I was just 22. When our third child, Kearstin, came along, I was only 27.

As many of us know, something happens when we reach our 30s. I hesitate to call it "maturity" because I've never seen myself as the mature type, but as we age, there seems to be a shift in our outlook on life and in our approach to parenting. This theory is confirmed whenever I think back to the way this mom handled certain things.

For instance, when our first child, Zac, was born, I decided that toy guns would be a no-no in our home. My husband, Ron, and I would be the people who would successfully raise a calm, sensitive, non-violent boy. That is until he turned three and I was giving him a bath with our one-year-old daughter,

Aubrey. Zac began making shooting noises at her while aiming the only weapon he had within grasp—his little man part. An hour later, I bought every plastic toy gun Dollar General had on its shelves.

No harm done, because a month later, I found him telling her to sit still while he gently held her head against the playroom wall. Apparently, he'd lost interest in guns and turned his attention to the exciting world of rubber cement. Thankfully, I found her before she dried.

When I became pregnant at the age of 35 with our fourth child Caymen, things were different from the get-go. As news of my pregnancy became public, the first question we were asked was always, "Was this an 'oops'?" That's a pretty natural assumption when your youngest is eight, but that only happened because it took me eight years to convince my husband to have his vasectomy reversed—another story for another time.

Starting over with a newborn at the age of 35 made me wonder, *How hard could it be? I'm a professional mom already.*

Soon after Caymen arrived, I realized I needed more sleep than I had when I was younger. How I made it to the age of 40 with a child who had her days and nights mixed up the first five years of her life is nothing short of a miracle.

Around Caymen's 18-month mark, the walls became an empty canvas for her crayons. In my exhausted state of mind, I would sigh and repaint the walls. Repeatedly. My other children never colored on the walls. They only glued each other to them. My "mom-sanity" was failing fast. *What's wrong with this fourth one?* I wondered.

I felt like a first-time parent. My only consolation was that potty training was around the corner, and Ron and I rocked at potty training.

For as many things as I feel I did wrong while parenting in my 20s, there's one thing I feel I did exactly right. (Indulge me as I pat myself on the back for a moment.) I was really good at potty training. When Zac was two and a half, we spent our summer days outside. I parked his potty chair by the back door, and our privacy fence allowed him to run free—meaning completely naked—around the yard. It took less than a week to get him trained.

I did the same thing with Aubrey and Kearstin, with the same success. So when Caymen turned two, we bought a potty chair in preparation for our potty-training boot camp that summer. But things did not go as planned.

Don't get me wrong—Caymen caught on to the potty feeling rather quickly. But she refused to use her potty chair and opted instead to hike her leg in the grass. While we were on vacation at the beach that summer, we were playing in the ocean when she told us she had to go potty. We told her to go potty in the water. (Don't act like you haven't done the same thing.) But instead, she walked out of the water and very obviously hiked her leg and peed on the sand—directly in front of the lifeguard.

As summer turned into fall and Caymen started going to the back door and asking to be let outside to go potty, I knew something had gone terribly wrong with my flawless system. I knew it was either the dog's fault or Ron's for both of their grass-peeing examples.

Regardless, I had exactly three years to rectify the situation before I had to explain to her kindergarten teacher she needed to be "let out" every couple of hours. It was time for me to undo the redneck damage and retrain the toddler.

Enter Pavlov. If he could train a puppy, so could I. Quick review: Ivan Pavlov became interested in the salivation habits of dogs. (Talk about someone with too much time on his hands.) He began ringing a little bell every time he would feed the dogs. After a while, the dogs began salivating to the sound of the bell whether food was in sight or not. So I came up with a plan.

I began sitting Caymen on her potty chair on a regular basis, and I made up a potty song to sing each time she did.

(To the tune of *Twinkle Twinkle Little Star*)

"Tinkle Tinkle Little Star,
Then you'll get a candy bar.
Put your potty in the chair,
Not in the grass or your underwear.
Tinkle Tinkle Little Star,
Then you'll get a candy bar."

In less than a week, it was working. I had to start buying candy bars in bulk, but it was worth it. Both her father and I sang that song everywhere—at church, in Walmart, at the doctor's office—you name it. Whenever Caymen was distracted by going potty in a new place, that song would send her into a potty trance and voilà!

Thus, this ditty has become my new advice for moms. But

as Pavlov could tell you, following up a tinkling sound with a treat has its side effects. Now I have to figure out how to get my daughter to stop salivating every time she goes to the bathroom.

Baby steps, people. Baby steps.

Caymen and Summer

Grazing Crazy O's

by
Renee Hughes

Intent on listening to the speaker, I jerked in my seat when something warm and solid brushed up my calves. Curious, I searched the floor around my feet and saw small hands picking at my legs. Upon bending all the way over, I found a tyke sprawled out on the floor, attempting to remove the dots from my textured pantyhose.

I turned and pointed at the boy to alert his parents. His dad retrieved him from the floor. "Oops, sorry," he apologized.

I wondered why parents were unable to control their kids. The answer to that question arrived a decade later after our son's birth.

My son's double overnight feedings exhausted me from the start. That should have been a clue Michael was going to be a hearty and frequent eater. Errands with him in tow required a fully stocked diaper bag. After Michael's teeth came in, I packed non-messy healthy treats, like dry cereal, to keep him happy and his tummy full.

On one trip, the two of us were going to attend a seminar. When we approached the building, a sign on the door forbade food, but I ignored it. Surely, the prohibition exempted nourishment for a toddler.

The event seating was in rows, and there were many of them. We chose seats near the rear of the building to allow for a quick exit, if needed.

Once we were settled in our seats, Michael rummaged through the diaper bag. He looked at me and quietly mouthed the words, "O's, Mama, O's."

But he was quick and found the plastic container before I did. Michael shook the container at me, which made the cereal rattle noisily. "O's, O's, O's!" he said aloud this time, drawing stares and knowing half-smiles from those seated nearby. Heat spread up my neck to my ears and cheeks after I realized we had morphed into the family with the nylon-dot-picking kiddo.

I quickly popped open the lid on the container, and my young son dug in, cramming a handful of cereal into his mouth. His nose wrinkled up, and then he sneezed. The muffled snort caught my attention because I suspected the results of that sound—flying debris.

A lady, who was impeccably dressed and had a massive bouffant, was seated directly in front of us. Her hair was styled so high that she must have used a half can of hairspray on it. But, unbeknownst to her, Michael's half-eaten O's now decorated the back of her voluminous, overteased and glued hairdo.

"O's, Mama," Michael said, just as he reached up to pick a piece of cereal off her head.

"No, don't," I admonished, handing him the container of cereal.

With my toddler redirected, I lightly plucked cereal from the back of the woman's head. Suddenly, in an abrupt motion on her part, she turned to stare at me. I smiled back innocently. Her eyes searched my face with suspicion then her head swiveled forward.

The retrieved cereal in my hand had escaped unnoticed. *She couldn't have felt my fingers tenderly harvesting the O's,* I worried to myself. I had never trusted those high-rise hairstyles—I knew they likely concealed something. An acquaintance once told me women inserted oatmeal boxes under the teased hair to reinforce the structures. *Maybe her hair has a life of its own and betrayed me, alerting her to my intrusion?*

Around us, muffled chuckles began to emanate from onlookers who had witnessed my initial cereal harvest. I motioned with an index finger over my lips to hush them. Embarrassed by my audience, I tried to discretely remove additional cereal, but the hair security alarm alerted the woman again. Louder giggles arose from those near us, so much so that I finally gave up.

After the event concluded, the woman stood up, and O's loosened from her bouffant. I guess the hair demons decided to reject the sticky cereal. O's confetti rained down as she paraded toward the exit in all her finery. *Yes! We have escaped discovery.*

That's when my eyes shifted downward in time to see

Michael following her, collecting freed cereal off the carpeting and popping the fallen O's into his mouth.

Mortified by Michael's floor grazing, I snatched him into my arms and pried open his mouth to extricate the contraband. He stuck his mush-covered tongue out at me, and then gave me a raspberry—bits of gummy O's sprayed all over my navy-blue dress. Michael flashed a toothy grin, evoking a spontaneous smile and headshake from me.

"If a 20-month-old can do this much damage," I muttered to myself, "what might the terrible twos hold in store?"

Why did I even ask?

Michael, age 3

You Just
Never Know

Expect the unexpected.

An Unforgettable Gaffe

by
Laura Graf

As any parent knows, traveling with kids can be a challenging adventure. There is always one child who needs to use the bathroom minutes after leaving the house, one who gets car sick, or one who tires quickly and wants to lie down. And of course there's all that bickering that goes on in the backseat.

As the mother of four children, I've learned to be prepared. I always fill a special bag with games, snacks, movies and special treats for good behavior to keep them busy and to discourage the whining and fighting that seems to go along with our road trips. However, nothing could have prepared me for a conflict over an action figure that led to one of my most embarrassing moments of motherhood.

It started out as a normal day on the road. It was the week before Christmas, and we were traveling to visit family. We'd packed the car with luggage and presents, and before leaving home, I'd instructed each one of my sons to pack a box of toys for the trip. Both had brought several of their favorite action figures.

We'd been on the road for a few hours; it seemed the ride was going to be enjoyable, as they were playing well together. However, it didn't take very long for them to reach their limit of brotherly love and togetherness. The mood and tone in the backseat began to change.

Looking in the rearview mirror, I noticed that the action figures were now spread out in disarray on the backseat. I couldn't help but wonder how many of those action figures would make it home with us and how many I would find under the seat or in the pockets on the door the next time I cleaned out the car.

"Give it back!" John, age nine, would say almost every five minutes. "Mom, Jesse has my guy!"

Minutes later, Jesse, age 11, complained, "John! Quit taking my guy! Mom, make him give it back to me!"

This went on for miles, with scuffling in the back seat and my turning around to demand that that they get along and stop taking each other's toys. Just as we had finished a long discussion on sharing and pulled into a gas station, I heard John's insistent voice. "Mom! Jesse has my guy again!"

At my wit's end, I opened the back door of the car and said, "Jesse! I've had enough of this! Give it to him now!"

"I don't have it. I swear!" declared Jesse, with the hint of a smile on his face.

"Yes, he does! Make him give it to me! He's hiding it!"

cried John again.

Frustrated beyond belief, I noticed something bulging in Jesse's pants. Poking the bulge, I demanded, "Really? What is that?!"

"What?" said Jesse, looking at me, confused.

Poking the bulge harder this time, I snapped, "That! Right there!"

"Uh . . ." replied Jesse with stunned amazement, "my penis?"

Imagine my shock and embarrassment! Deciding there was nothing I could do to save face or settle the argument, I quickly closed the door and retreated to the gas pump, praying this would be one childhood memory my son would forget.

The Consummate Performer

by
Kathryn Cureton

My youngest son is quite the consummate performer. That his talents are not those in high demand for a second-grade musical performance has never crossed his mind. The boy is an absolute angel at home.

And his grades have always been exemplary. Sure, there was that little business of his refusing to obey the substitute gym teacher during kindergarten, and the resulting trip to visit the assistant principal.

"What did the principal say to you?"

"Nothing."

"What did you say to the principal?"

"Nothing."

"Do you mean to tell me that you both just sat there and

looked at each other?"

"No. I was standing up."

I'm sure he was just bored when he threw his pencil across the art room and was told he would need to apologize or visit the assistant principal again. After all, it was a victimless crime. As he said, "I never would have gotten caught if my whole table hadn't told on me."

Even when he came home with his jean pockets full of yarn balls, I was willing to give him the benefit of the doubt.

"Where did you get those?"

"From the art teacher."

"He gave you all those yarn balls?"

"Uh huh. He said everybody could have one."

"You have a lot more than one."

"They were sitting in a jar on his desk. And he said I could have one. He wasn't even watching. So I took them."

I should have paid more attention to the warning signs. Sure, his bus driver told him to sit in the front seat, but I thought that was to protect him from the big kids. His teachers provided me with more foreshadowing than a Stephen King novel: the afternoon drop-in visits to my own classroom to apprise me of his progress; the sight of him sitting alone on the first bleacher during the run-though on the afternoon of the Christmas program, guarded by a single faculty member.

It's not like he was a terror. A bully. A common thief of anything besides yarn balls.

He didn't even want to be in the Christmas program. But it was part of his grade. And everybody knows that second-grade music is part of the permanent record that follows you out into the world when you graduate. So we told him he was going, and that was that.

My husband and I kept him with us in the bleachers until the last minute. That way, he wouldn't run wild beforehand and work up a good head of steam prior to the performance. We had a talk about his behavior. Promises were made. He promised to be good. He vowed to make me proud, not embarrassed. I promised I would take away his Game Boy for a week if he acted up. We all agreed to the terms.

His dad took him to the staging area in the band room five minutes before showtime. I saved my husband's seat from latecomers intent on worming their way onto the front row. Somehow, we felt that we could control our boy's behavior if we were in close proximity.

We were giddy with anticipation. Second and third graders marched out of the hallway and into the gym. My first inkling of what was to come was my boy's position in the 160-member choir. He was in the center of the first row, carefully packaged between four girls on one side and two girls on the other. He walked out like a little gentleman, hands in the pockets of his dress pants. His grandma gushed, "Oh, he's being so good."

The choir climbed onto the risers, three rows high. My son was on the front row, directly in front of the choir teacher. They sang the first song then sat down. My boy fit right in. But wait! There were still six songs left, and in between, four acts of the Frosty-the-Snowman play that some well-behaved kids got to perform. My son couldn't see the play from where he was sitting. I thought to myself, *I'm sure he must be gifted, which would explain his short attention span.*

The little girl on his right wore a long Christmas dress. He put his shoe on the bottom of her dress. She gathered it up and pulled it around her legs. He lifted her dress and poked at her shoes. She gave him the cold shoulder.

He pulled up his pants legs past the knee, one by one, until he looked like he was wearing a tan, corduroy Speedo. He tugged his black socks up to his knees. He admired them. He put his pants legs back down.

Time for a song. They stood up. He gave the girl on his right the bunny ears. He gave the girl on his left the bunny ears. He gave them both the bunny ears at once. *Talented, that boy of mine.*

His dad was giving him the "stop it" sign, like an umpire spreads out his arms to say "safe." I frowned and shook my head. Oh, he saw us, all right. The giveaway was that little grin. A grin that said, "Oh, but the night is mine, Mother and Father, for you cannot come out here onto the gym floor. There is a musical program in progress, you see. And I am the center of attention."

A fifth-grade teacher sat next to my husband. She thought it was hilarious. She knew she was safe for three more years.

The choir sat down again. My boy picked at some dried Silly String on the plastic that lined the gym floor. It was left over from a senior class several years ago that did not obey the principal's graduation ceremony command of "No Silly String. It will ruin our brand-new gym floor liner." The custodians struggled for a week to remove the petrified string. They tried every cleaner imaginable. Silly custodians! All they had to do was bring in a crew of second graders and say, "Now, don't touch that Silly String."

My boy began to kick his foot. Because he was wearing loafers, or his "churchy shoes" as he called them, his right shoe sailed through the air and crashed to the floor about 15 feet away. The music teacher didn't even flinch when it shot past her head—she kept right on directing that choir with gusto. But she did give him the stink-eye without missing a beat.

He got up to get his shoe. He karate-chopped himself in the genital region. He opened his mouth wide and rolled his eyes. On the next song, he kicked his feet, kind of like a chorus-line dancer, only not as high. "He's just dancing with the music," said his father, the eternal optimist.

"He's trying to kick off his shoe again!" I told him. *Men can be so clueless!*

Song over. Another act of the play. My son leaned back and blindly karate-chopped the boy behind him. His second-grade teacher popped up from behind the risers like a behavior-patrol jack-in-the-box. She appeared to hiss a warning. My boy turned his attention back to the girl with the long dress. He slowly pulled her belt from around her waist and grandly presented it to her with a flourish. She snatched it out of his hands.

The choir stood for the next song. My boy leaned over the girl on his other side, his face at her midsection. He pretend-sniffed the flower on her frock. She pushed his head away. He smirked. The song ended, and they sat again.

By now, my boy was running out of steam. He picked his nose. With both hands. He persuaded the girl on his right to pick at the Silly String. Mercifully, the program ended.

He looked worried as my husband went to retrieve him. His teacher stepped up. "Your son is really improving."

My boy swaggered over to me and said, "I'll take my Game Boy now."

"Uh, no, you won't. You can't have it back until the weekend."

That did not go over well. He pouted all the way home.

"Didn't you see us telling you to stop acting up?"

"No. I saw Dad make this sign." He demonstrated it perfectly.

"Then why didn't you stop?"

He heaved a heavy sigh. "Uh . . . the sign for 'stop it' is this." He made a chopping motion with one hand onto the other—the American Sign Language sign. Perhaps his entire attention-getting repertoire could have been avoided if only my husband and I were fluent in American Sign Language.

Nah. I seriously doubt it.

A Day at the Theater

by
Angela Thomas

Children, God love them. Some leave us beaming with pride, while others cause us to apologize before taking them anywhere.

But no matter how our children behave, we love them anyway. Mothers start parenting school with a diaper bag in hand and graduate to the well-known "mom bag," which always seems to weigh more than a two-year-old toddler.

As a mother of young daughters, I had learned quickly to prepare for any mishap. That meant I had to load an arsenal of kids' survival tools into my purse and carry the typical mom bag over my already-burdened shoulders. Prior to each outing, I ran through a routine that would pass any Army drill sergeant's inspection. Wipes, check; extra clothing, check; snacks, check. The list went on and on.

One particular day, I heard there was to be a special showing of

Steven Spielberg's 1982 megahit movie, *E.T. the Extra-Terrestrial*, at the local theater. Having missed it the first time around, I did not want to miss it again. After all, Spielberg had cast two young actors in the film who were a little older than my daughters, Heather and Amber. I thought these young actors might fascinate them.

We arrived at the theater to find the lobby turned into a wonderland of E.T. memorabilia. Large cutouts of a cute extra-terrestrial were scattered about, and there were tables filled with cups, lunch boxes, posters and everything imaginable with E.T.'s image plastered on it. My children were in heaven and eager to see the movie.

Before the movie started, we made our routine stop at the restroom, "just in case," and stopped by the concession stand for popcorn and soda. It didn't take long for us to find the perfect seats for a clear view of the giant movie screen. When the lights began to fade and the previews began to play, both daughters squirmed in their seats from excitement.

Their excitement grew when they saw the young actors on the screen, and even more so when E.T. appeared. Heather asked loudly, "Mom, is it real?" Amber, my youngest daughter, wasn't sure what to believe. Both were in awe of E.T. and captivated by the special effects throughout the movie.

As the movie progressed, Amber, who normally was the most talkative of the two, turned silent. No more squirming, no more interaction with her sister—nothing.

When the movie went into the third act and the suspense began to build, the moviegoers—adults and children alike—were silent. One could hear a pin drop. Suddenly, Amber yelled out, "Mommy, I want to go hooooome!"

"Quiet," I whispered in her ear. "You can't yell out like that."

"Mommy, take me home!" she yelled again. Suddenly, she got up from her seat and began projectile vomiting like I had never seen before. I quickly grabbed her hand and headed up the aisle for the nearest restroom. As I was leaving, I told Heather to stay seated, ensuring her I'd be back.

As we made our way up the aisle, Amber stopped several times, screaming and spewing vomit. The low lighting on the aisle helped me to guide her out of the theater, but before reaching the door, I could hear several people gagging.

"Mommy, wait! Mommy, don't leave me in the dark!" Heather shouted. She raced up the aisle to catch up with us, slipping and falling in vomit. An usher came to my aid to help me through the door.

I was embarrassed. We reached the restroom where Amber continued to vomit, scream and cry while her sister sobbed with big, heaving motions. I took them to the sink and cleaned them up as best I could. I reached into my bag, grabbed the extra clothing and changed them quickly before heading back into the lobby.

When we stepped into the lobby, the theater doors were open and the lights had been turned up. Several mothers with children raced toward the restroom with evidence of vomit on their clothing. Whether they were sick themselves or had slipped on Amber's vomit in the aisle, I'll never know, but each mother gave me the evil eye as they passed by.

I learned before leaving that the movie had been stopped. I couldn't decide if the humiliation was greater than the experience, but to tell you the truth, we never returned to that theater. Days following the movie fiasco, Amber asked if we could go see *E.T.* again. I guess you know what my answer was.

Through all of the dramas, embarrassments and crying fits, somehow, we mothers survive. From diaper bags to "mom bags" and beyond, we'll look back on our most humiliating moments and remember them fondly.

Class Clown

by
Stacey Gustafson

Parent-teacher conferences are as unsettling as being attacked on a city street by a flock of geese overdosed on Ex-Lax. You hope you don't get hit with something you weren't expecting.

When our son brought home a crumpled-up reminder note about his upcoming parent-teacher conference, my husband said to me, "Should we be concerned?"

"Nah," I said with a laugh. "We've got nothing to fear. Our little guy is fun-loving, smart and inquisitive. He's right on track." I was certain his bubbly kindergarten teacher would load on the compliments with a flash of her professionally whitened teeth and say, "Your son is fabulous. A model student."

This would be a piece of cake.

I prepared a list of questions for Ms. Smiley, such as, "Is our child working to the best of his ability? Is he a visual, auditory or tactile learner?"

The day of the conference, we peeked at the parent-teacher appointment list taped on the classroom door and confirmed it was the correct room at the right time. My husband and I entered the classroom with a grin and took a seat. The perky, young teacher beamed down at us from her stool, hands folded in her lap.

Let the bragging begin.

With a serious face, she said, "I love your son's energy. He is certainly enthusiastic, but . . ."

No buts. Please . . . no buts, I thought, my heart starting to race.

She continued, "But yard duty volunteers are concerned he's causing a commotion at recess. Personally, I embrace his enthusiasm."

Whew!

"What's he doing?" I asked.

"He has single-handedly taught the whole kindergarten class how to armpit fart. No worries. I think boys should be boys," she said with a giggle.

At the doorway, a woman with a deep voice cleared her throat and said, "When you're finished here, do you mind dropping by the gymnasium?" and scooted off with a flash of spiky, black hair.

"Who's that?" I asked his teacher.

"Your son's physical education instructor, Ms. Wagner. Not sure what she wants," she said with a twist of her ponytail. "As I was saying, he's a pleasure to have in class. Mom and Dad, you're doing a good job."

You bet we are!

I winked at my husband and gripped his hand as we strutted down the hallway to the gym. The teacher straightened the exercise mats and flagged us over to her corner office.

"Thanks for coming by," she said, running a hand through her hair. "I want to start out by saying that I enjoy having your son in class, but I'm concerned about his safety and the well-being of the other kids."

Woman, what are you talking about?

"He's the biggest boy in class, and I'm afraid he's going to hurt the other children."

"What's he doing?" I said with a frown.

"Let me give you an example. Right now the class is doing gymnastics, practicing log rolls and somersaults on the mats. Yesterday, he rolled across his mat, knocked down the other children then rolled over their bodies and out the gymnasium door," she said, rubbing the back of her neck. "We're concerned about his safety."

Oh, my God! He's like a human Army tank!

"I don't want to take up any more of your time," she said, pushing back her chair and standing up. "Please try to get your kid under control."

With weak handshakes and our heads held in shame, we left the gym. As we rushed down the hallway to get the hell out of there, a tall, bearded man with fashionable glasses blocked our way. "Glad I bumped into you," he said, looking us up and down. "I'm your son's music teacher, Mr. Thompson. Can you stop by for 30 seconds?"

"Uh . . . sure," we said in unison.

Oh boy, our son is a musical prodigy!

Once in the music room, we plopped down on the metal risers next to the teacher. "First, I want to tell you that your child has a very high level of energy."

"OK," I said, sneaking a look at my husband.

"He's disrupting the class," he blurted out.

"Can you give us an example?"

"Let me show you," he said as he hoisted himself up in true dramatic fashion. We stared, eyes wide and mouths open, as a 6-foot 3-inch giant hopped around the classroom like a one-legged kangaroo and slapped his butt with wooden drumsticks.

We departed the room holding onto each other, unable to suppress the laughter any longer. I glanced over my shoulder and spied the teacher as he chuckled and dabbed his eyes with a tissue.

Geez, our son, the five-year-old class clown!

Clowning around (again)

Throwing in the Towel

by
Debra Mayhew

When I was a kid, I thought my mom had the strangest laundry system. Her washer and dryer were in the basement, in a large room with a concrete floor. There was plenty of space for the hot water heater, a couple of freezers, canning shelves, a utility sink and a table for folding clothes. So Mom took an old playpen, opened it up and positioned it directly under the laundry chute.

Soon enough, the playpen was heaped to overflowing and bulging at the sides with dirty clothes and the occasional Barbie doll or library book. Once in a while, all the clothes would get emptied, sorted, washed, folded and put away. But for the most part, we rarely saw the bottom of the playpen.

I was secretly disdainful of this. *Really,* I wondered, *how hard is it to stay caught up on laundry?* So what if she had seven children and about a hundred things to take care of each day?

She was a mom, and these were the kinds of things moms were supposed to get done. Right?

I decided I would do a better job when I became a mom. I was determined to have a more efficient laundry system. Dirty clothes weren't going to pile up on me. My kids wouldn't have to fight each other for the last pair of clean underwear. My dishtowels weren't going to grow mold in the time it took to get them bleached and back to the kitchen.

All that changed when I got married and started my own family. For a few years, I did pretty well. I stuck to a schedule and rarely fell behind. I remember thinking, *See? It's not that hard. Anyone can stay caught up on laundry if they have the right system.*

My reality check arrived about the same time our fourth child was born. There I was, mom and laundress to four children under the age of six. Those were some happy days, to be sure, but they were also some messy days. I cared less and less about laundry and more and more about living. The dirty clothes had a funny way of multiplying overnight and hiding in nooks and crannies all over my house. Occasionally, they even held a pile of clean, folded clothes hostage in their crumpled mounds.

But I didn't care. Plus, I was beginning to understand the logic in Mom's wacky system. As my To-Do list got longer and longer, the laundry got bumped further and further down the list. Before long, keeping up seemed almost laughable.

I adopted a new motto: It's not a mom's job to do all the work, but just to make sure the work gets done. As the kids grew, they were tasked with hauling dirty clothes and switching loads.

I whittled their wardrobes down to a week's worth of outfits and donated the excess. I stopped pre-treating stains and eliminated ironing altogether.

I still couldn't keep up, but I was making peace with my imperfect system. Or so I thought.

Then last December a strange thing happened. My 10-year-old son Daniel was scheduled to get some dental work done. Because I was recuperating from a cesarean section and tending a newborn, my husband took him to his appointment.

I wasn't out of bed when they left that morning, so I didn't see the clothes Daniel was wearing. If I had, I would've ordered him to change immediately. But my husband doesn't pay attention to those kinds of things, and he didn't notice the stained sweatshirt, wrinkled pants and dirty socks our son wore. So off they went.

Daniel is a chatty kid, so I imagine he got comfortable in the chair and had a rather pleasant morning while they worked on his teeth. I can also imagine that the dentist must've thought Daniel needed more than just some help with his teeth because of what happened next.

When the dentist was done, she took my husband aside and said quietly, "I'd like to give you something so you can buy Daniel a Christmas gift." She had obviously noticed Daniel's less-than-tidy appearance and assumed we could use some help with his care.

My husband was surprised to see her offering $15. He shook his head. "That's very nice of you," he said with a smile, "but you don't have to do it."

"Please," she insisted. "I want to do it."

He was a little embarrassed, but knew she meant well, so he took the money, came home and told me the story.

Daniel walked in the door with a sparkly smile, and I got my first glimpse of his grubby outfit. "Daniel! Why did you have to go out looking like that?" I asked.

He looked down at his clothes with a puzzled expression. "What's wrong with it?"

"That shirt!" I pointed. "It's got stains all over it! And look at your pants! They look terrible!"

"But, Mom!" he said, "These are my favorite clothes!"

I shook my head and sighed, feeling like the worst mom ever. Laundry had bested me yet again.

But then I noticed the silver lining and had to smile. This was the first time I was paid for falling behind on laundry.

L to R: Debra, mom Eileen and her sister Elizabeth

Keeping It Real

by
Erika Hoffman

When my children were young, I decided to run for the county's school board.

I taught school for several years before becoming the mother of four. Even after I left teaching to raise my family, I stayed abreast of school issues. Many of my closest friends had remained teachers after becoming parents, and I visited with them weekly at the local high school.

During those weekly visits in my small North Carolina town, I visited with cosmetology students while they styled my hair. I listened to their concerns. We discussed the usual problems, and of course drug use was one of them.

At community meetings, I addressed not only the problems of drug use, but also more specific concerns. I had a vision of what I would like to see accomplished. That's why I decided to run for an opening on the county school board. Unfortunately, my vision wasn't the same as that of most of the voters. In my heart, I knew I had little chance of winning the election.

My friends suggested I network more. My opponents—both men—were faithful churchgoers and popular in their respective communities. Both had full congregations behind them, as well as their respective political parties.

Both as a child and a teen, I had faithfully attended church every Sunday, as well as attending youth group get-togethers Sunday nights. During college, my commitment waned. But after I married, moved to a small town and had my first child, I felt the pull to join a place of worship. I rediscovered organized religion. I wanted to become a part of the community.

Yet, because my husband worked Sundays, I had to attend church without him. As the number of our offspring kept increasing, getting ready for church became harder and harder. I had to feed them, dress them and myself in our Sunday best and make it out the door before the final "Amen."

Now that I was running for political office for the first time in my life, with less than a glimmer of a chance of gaining the seat, I felt it imperative for the townsfolk to know that I valued religion, even though I'd never win any church-attendance pin. To make matters worse, I wasn't a North Carolinian native. I hailed from the Northeast, about 20 miles outside of New York City. My husband, a born-and-bred Southerner of countless generations, reminded me, "Do you know what people down here say is the difference between a Yankee and a damn Yankee?"

"What?"

"A Yankee visits. A damn Yankee stays."

That joke is good for a few guffaws. Trouble is, like anything that makes a person laugh, it's funny because there's a smidgen of truth to it. Ergo, I wanted these North Carolinian folks—my adopted, extended family—to realize I was one of them! So, on Mother's Day, sans Southern spouse, I showed up for the Methodist service with my brood in tow.

That Mother's Day, I secretly hoped there'd be some recognition for the parent with the most kids at church instead of the annual honor to the oldest and the youngest moms. I was 36—too long-in-the-tooth to be the youngest mommy and, given my gene pool, unlikely ever to become an octogenarian. Everyone in this congregation was blessed with Methuselah's DNA. Several 90-plusers perched in the pews in front of me. In fact, on this particular Mother's Day, I'd never seen so many white heads, blue heads and even some sort of blond hue on ladies over the age when there's no way the shade could be mistaken as natural.

Because I had thrown my hat into the political arena, I felt as if the eyes of the congregants were riveted on me. My five-month-old daughter squirmed in my lap. My two-and-a-half-year-old boy snuggled up on one side of me, and his four-year-old and six-year-old brothers fidgeted on my other flank. I threatened them before the service. I also made extravagant promises. I promised that, after the service, I would buy anything they wanted if they'd not talk or yell or cry or make any noise whatsoever during the ritual. I practiced psychology on them, too. I told them how smart and well-behaved they were and how all the church folks considered them bright and would be observing their excellent manners. "Every mommy will wish she had you four youngins as kids, because you will be so good today," I announced to them before we entered the nave.

I wore a yellow silk dress. My little girl looked adorable in her polka-dot bonnet and matching attire. I held her up on my shoulder. She cried a bit. I shifted shoulders. When I glanced back at my two-year-old son seated next to me, I saw the epaulette of spit-up where my daughter had been drooling, and then I noticed the second epaulette of residue forming where she now rested. I folded her onto my lap as I discreetly wiped off the white gob. My toddler whined for his bottle then gulped it loudly. We stood to sing.

I can't recall the order of the program or when I first realized my four-year-old and six-year-old boys were missing. I looked down the pew to my left. No kids. To my right. No kids. I craned my neck. I wasn't able to wield my entire torso easily since my daughter, like an anchor on my lap, restricted my pivoting. A few sweet church ladies beamed at my baby and cooed at her. I smiled. We bowed our heads for prayer.

I felt I should excuse myself to hunt down my errant sons, but I reasoned they must have escaped out the back door, and I'd collect them in a minute after the minister finished his prayer. Suddenly, in the rows in front of me, I observed old dowagers straighten up quickly and say aloud, "Oh!" or "Oh, my!" Soon, a chorus of startled murmurs followed.

"Whoo! What was that?" I heard one huff. Surprised noises filled the sanctuary as these stooped ladies kicked up their arthritic legs to make room for my two offspring, who were rolling down the slanted floor under the pews like human logs, banging into limbs that moved or lifted to make way for their egress. I don't know if my eyes formed saucers or whether I turned blushing red or sick-to-my-stomach green. I felt the nerves beneath my right eye convulse involuntarily. I became woozy and hot and wanted to vanish into the woodwork.

I didn't see my two Muppets until their little heads popped up in front of the altar just as our reverend was about to pronounce, "Amen." I swooped up my baby. She spewed more liquid down the back of my dress. I grabbed my toddler fiercely with the other hand and lifted him, airborne, from the wooden seat. We zoomed down the aisle, half flying, as I felt heads swivel toward us. I heard the whispers mount. When I reached the altar, I glared at my impish boys and mouthed: "Time to go." They laughed and scooted through the swinging doors to the back staircase.

"Is church over, Mom?" the six year old asked happily, jumping down the stairs two at a time.

I nodded.

"Now it's time for our reward!" he said, looking expectant.

They followed me as I stormed to the parking lot. I buckled the baby in her infant contraption and strapped the two-year-old behind her, as my two other sons fought over the "shotgun" seat. On the way home, I informed them it was Mother's Day, and I didn't think I was a very good mother because they didn't sit quietly and behave in church, even after I had warned them repeatedly. They listened half-heartedly.

After we had pulled into the driveway, my anger was spent, and I took the little ones inside where I put the baby into the crib and the toddler into his highchair. I sat at the kitchen table with my head in my hands. This wasn't the Mother's Day I'd anticipated when I laid out their outfits the night before. I realized then that I didn't need a seat on the school board. I needed to figure out how to be the mom I wanted to be at home.

My rascally boys barged through the door with a bunch of flowers they'd picked from a neighbor's garden and thrust them in front of my nose. They looked proud of themselves, just as they had when they had rolled under the pews all the way down to the minister's feet earlier that morning.

I put my arms around them. "You are two little characters." Then, it dawned on me: I am a mother—not a perfect mother, not one who will ever win any award or get elected to any office, but I have what counts. I wanted a family of stair-step kids. I have that family! With a group like mine, embarrassment might do me in, but I'll never die of boredom.

I didn't win that school board seat. I never ran again for any office. That was over a quarter of a century ago, and I have no regrets. My four kids grew up to be successful yet grounded, ambitious yet amusing and respectable. But by all accounts, they are still characters!

Erika and her children at the time of the story

Off the Hook

by
Nancy Julien Kopp

I glanced at the clock, tapped my foot for the nth time and hollered up the stairway, "C'mon, Kirk. We need to get going."

My 11-year-old son had been to the dentist for an early-morning appointment, and I needed to get him to school. I, ready to holler once again, grabbed my coat that had been lying across a kitchen chair. Before I could manage it, Kirk came bounding down the stairs, grabbed his winter coat and sailed by me, out to the car in the garage. I followed right on his heels.

Backing down the driveway, I was in full mom mode. "Where's your hat? It's freezing outside, and you have no hat to wear out on the playground. How bright is that?"

Silence.

Turning the corner at a reckless speed because of my angst, I added the final barb. "I don't want you home with pneumonia again." Visions of one very sick boy must have entered both our heads, but neither of us commented.

More silence.

Finally, Kirk blurted a response. "Mom, hats mess up my hair!"

Exasperated, I retorted quicker than a jackrabbit runs across the Arizona desert. "Big deal! Lots of days my hair doesn't behave the way I want it to. But you know what? Life goes on."

His response came even faster. "Yeah, but you've already got a husband."

We'd reached the school. I slowed to a stop, and Kirk jumped out, slamming the door in a final response.

I drove home in a minor stupor. *What just happened?* I wondered. My little boy had taken a leap onto the bottom rung of the ladder to manhood. He'd rather freeze his ears on the playground than risk his hair being messed up. He wanted to look his best for the girls in his class.

Wow! My child is growing up. Am I ready for this new stage?

When school was over and Kirk came home, neither of us mentioned our less-than-friendly conversation earlier in the day. But I looked at him with a new perspective. *Girls on his mind? What does he know about girls and boys or the birds and the bees? Who should talk to him? Is this the right time?*

I discussed the predicament with my husband, Ken, later that night, but he didn't offer to do the deed. Ken was a good dad who provided well for his family, but he much preferred that the responsibility of disciplining and caring for the children fall to me. Easy for him, not so for me.

Life went on for several weeks of cold winter days with

a boy who would wear no hat. I didn't nag him, but I thought a lot about how I was going to have the talk with him. I remembered when I'd found out about sex—in sixth grade on the playground. Beverly, a student whose dad was a doctor, gathered all the girls around her and said she had something to tell us. She proceeded to inform her captive audience of all the physical aspects of how babies came to be.

Of course, more than half of us told her she was crazy. Our parents would never do such a thing. Never! Beverly put her hands on her hips and narrowed her eyes. "I read it in one of my father's medical books. It's all true." She turned on her heel and ran all the way to the school, while the rest of us stood there totally tongue-tied. I doubt much schoolwork was done that afternoon, with those mental images racing through the minds of all the sixth-grade girls.

Now, it would be my turn to inform someone—my own little boy—about the mechanics of creation. I let even more days go by. I was one big chicken. Finally, I knew I had to be a mom and have the talk. I went upstairs to say goodnight to Kirk and his little sister Karen. I stopped by the pink room first, tucked Karen in and kissed her forehead.

Then it was on to the blue room, where my son had just slipped into bed. I sat on the edge of his bed and said, "Kirk, maybe we should have a talk about babies and girls and boys and all that stuff." *Oh great,* I thought. *What a namby-pamby way to begin. What should I say next?*

Kirk pulled the comforter up around his shoulders and said, "Oh, you don't have to do that, Mom. Artie and Matt already told me all about it." He turned on his side and said no more.

Artie and Matt were two boys on our block who were about four years older than Kirk. They were the oldest boys in the neighborhood, and the younger kids looked up to them. I wanted to ask Kirk if he'd told them his mother and father would never, ever do THAT like my girlfriends and I had told Beverly. Instead, I leaned over and kissed his cheek and pushed the hair off his forehead before I headed downstairs.

I got as far as the doorway before I turned around and said, "Kirk, if you have any questions, you know you can come to me or Dad and ask. You do know that, don't you?"

A muffled "Yes" was all I got for an answer.

A little giggle started way down in my stomach and made its way upward until it became a full-blown laugh by the time I hit the bottom step. When I got to the family room, I was still laughing.

Ken looked away from the TV. "What's so funny?" he asked.

I got control of myself then answered, "It seems we owe Artie and Matt a thank you. They instructed Kirk and some other boys about how babies are made. Got us both off the hook."

Did I dare write the incident in his baby book? After all, I put in a little report on the first tooth, first haircut, first words. Somehow, I doubted there would be a page heading that said, "First Sex Instruction."

Raise My Glass

by
Kristi Stephens Walker

I really like the song *Raise Your Glass* by Pink. On a busy Friday morning a few weeks ago, that soundtrack played in my head as I got my kids ready for school.

I admit that I did, indeed, take the kids to school in my pajamas that day. My reasoning was that I would drive them around the building and through the drop-off line without having to get out of the car. Boy, was I wrong!

It wasn't just my sparkling personality that made me stand out that morning—it was also the purple flannel polka-dotted pajama bottoms I wore, the long-sleeved T-shirt, the red-and-black wool socks and the burgundy flats. I topped the whole ensemble with a super-cute navy sweater-wrap, the *pièce de ré-sistance,* in an effort to salvage my dignity.

As I approached the railroad tracks near my home, I was stopped by Nashville's single commuter train, the Music City Star. That's when I realized my dignity was headed for a train wreck—we would not be on time and I would have to walk the kids into school.

It's not that I wanted to avoid yet another letter from the truancy office. Sure, I care about my kids' education, and promptness is a part of that responsibility when learning. Yeah, I get all that crap. I just wanted to get my kids there before I received another shaming look from front-office-staffer and all-around-keeper-of-the-keys—Mrs. Shamey McTardimuggins.

But pajamas and all, it was my lucky day! Because a la Pink, I was, as she says in her song, "too school for cool." Imagine my delight when I screeched to a halt in front of the school and ushered my kids out of the car, one of whom was still finishing off a French toast stick and a swig of juice, to find the school's front doors still open. That meant no sign-in! That meant no shaming looks! No tardy today! But the kids would have to hurry—the door was about to close.

"Ha ha, suckas!" I shouted to the people pulling into the parking lot. These were the fully dressed people with dignity still intact, whom I'd zoomed passed in my late fury, humming *Raise Your Glass* the whole way.

It was then that I noticed our beloved, highly professional and erudite principal at the front door, greeting the last of the on-time children with an equally professional-looking guest. And there I was, secretary of the PTA board, in my flannels. I considered a swan dive into the landscaping and an Army crawl back to the van, but I thought the principal had already spotted me.

So I mustered what was left of my self-respect and stood up straight, cinching up my sweater-wrap. I waved gracefully and kissed the kids goodbye. "Have a great day, kids! Mommy promises to be dressed when I pick you up after school, unless I get caught up in a *Glee* marathon this afternoon."

Back in the safety of my van, I was thrilled to find that one of my children had left her freshly poured juice in the car. She loves to drink her juice out of a tiny wineglass she calls the "fancy glass." I grabbed it and took a long drink of the pineapple-orange juice. I was trying to merge in front of a gentleman driving a huge, red truck, who had no doubt watched my pajama-clad freak show only moments before.

Perhaps I'd frightened him. Maybe he was being nice. Maybe he wondered why the hell PTA Mom was dropping kids off in her jammies and swilling what appeared to be mimosas from a wineglass at 8 o'clock in the morning.

Whatever his reason, he kindly motioned for me to go ahead, and I did the only thing I could think of.

I raised my glass to him.

CHAPTER FOUR

Yes, I'm Your Mother

And I'm one in a million!

One Mom's Crowning Moment

by
Jill Pertler

More and more, my life borders on the edge of absurdity.

Last night, I paraded around the house with an athletic cup on my head, waiting for someone to notice. You read that right.

For those of you unfamiliar with sports equipment and terminology, I'm not referring to a vessel for drinking Gatorade. The cup in question is one that provides protection to male athletes where—some would say—they need it most.

What would drive a grown woman to wear an athletic cup on her head?

In my case, it was another cup, which I had found lying on the living-room couch. For many of you, having an athletic protector on your couch might be considered absurd, but in my house, well, let's just say it isn't.

I found the couch-cup and decided to determine the identity of its owner. My two oldest sons—both likely prospects—denied any knowledge of the item in question. After further interrogation, they revealed they could only find one athletic protector between the two of them, so they'd been sharing! Again, an absurd idea in some households. Unfortunately, not in mine.

I knew in my heart we were a multiple-cup family and initiated a hunt for the missing equipment. Within 30 seconds, I'd found an extra two right where I'd put them on laundry day—lying front and center in the boys' sock drawer.

This is when the absurdity of it all overwhelmed me. I found the situation wickedly hilarious, so I strapped one of the clean cups over my head and marched around the house.

It took longer than you'd imagine for my boys to notice. This didn't surprise me.

I live in a family populated by males. While I love my guys dearly, they are lacking in what I term "scanning ability." This deficiency helps explain their failure to locate the extra cups in the first place.

The same can be said for any number of household items. For instance, if I move the ketchup to a different location in the fridge, they assume we are out of ketchup and are simply willing to eat their fries without it. They never think to give the fridge a quick once-over in case the ketchup is hiding behind the chocolate milk. They don't consider looking in the pantry for a new bottle.

While they will take the time to tell me we are out of

ketchup, they won't spend one millisecond looking for it. The same, apparently, goes for athletic cups and numerous other items including, but not limited to, toothpicks, masking tape, permission slips, flashlights, hockey jerseys, toilet paper, socks, library books, favorite T-shirts, shampoo, mittens, baseball hats, homework, toothbrushes, pencils, the garbage can and underwear.

I know I should push more for them to cultivate their scanning abilities, but it's an uphill battle. If my husband is any indication, my boys are genetically predisposed with an inability to scan.

So nine times out of 10, I—begrudgingly—scan for the missing items. Some might call me an enabler. Others will see me as gullible or a pushover.

While all these might be true, I've created a different name for myself. I am "Supreme Locator, Finder of All That is Needed." My title even comes with a few perks, including a crown, which, to some, might resemble an athletic cup.

My Beaver

by
Shayla Seay

When I gave birth to my son Zacch at age 23, I thought I was young to be having a child. A single mother, I didn't have a job or own a car, and I didn't even have a penny in the bank. I was in the middle of nowhere with nothing but the knowledge my parents and the world had instilled in my then-young mind. As it turned out, that was all I needed to raise a good child.

The values my parents taught me were important. Every vacation, weekend camping trip or party my family hosted was a lesson in life. I learned cleanliness, politeness, etiquette, appreciation, generosity, compliance, a strong work ethic and many other values that made me what I am today.

The most important lesson I took away from my childhood was appreciation; whether we were rich or poor, I wanted to teach Zacch to be decent and thankful for whatever he had. If I could do that, I knew my only child would turn out fine.

When Zacch was three, I began teaching him thankfulness by showing him how to write thank you cards. At Christmas, Zacch scribbled notes in green and red crayon that we would send along to his grandma and grandpa, aunties and uncles. The older he got, the better and longer the notes became.

Three years later, I started Zacch on writing apology notes to friends he might have upset, babysitters he had unnerved and even to me for things about which I felt he needed to apologize. As a parent, I knew that writing a note, along with a verbal recognition, would cause Zacch to spend more time reflecting on his behavior. Granted, anyone can say "Thank you" over the phone or "I'm sorry" in person, but having to write it down made it more meaningful. Putting words on paper took those words from one dimension to 3-D, and it gave Zacch something to think about instead of something that just rolled off the tip of his tongue.

Once when Zacch was seven, he raised his voice to me. Earlier in the day, he had gotten into trouble in school and when he got home, he talked back to me. I, of course, sent him to his room with no television or video games, but only with his thoughts, his pencils and some paper to keep him company.

That evening, I took Zacch's dinner to his room. Setting the plate down next to him, I didn't say a word, but simply turned around and walked out. I imagined he thought I was still upset, but, in truth, I was smiling. When I entered his room, I saw that my boy had picked up that one important value I had taught him—he was writing me a note.

When I awoke the next morning, I noticed the note had been slipped under my door. It read:

> *To Mom, I'm sorry for my beaver today. I hope you can for give me. My beaver wus realy realy bad and disrespetful to you. I am realy stuped today I dun now why but I Love You. Love Zacch*

I framed the note and hung it outside Zacch's bedroom door. Everyone who reads it laughs aloud. Even though Zacch is now 19 and in the U.S. Navy, he still becomes embarrassed when he sees it. And to this day, I have never had anyone else tell me, "I'm sorry for my beaver." Apology accepted.

Thrill Ride

by
Camille Subramaniam

Turbulence tossed our plane like a tin can in the wind. The fasten-seat-belt sign flashed on with a ding. We would land in Bali's international airport in 20 minutes.

My husband had planned this vacation during an annual trip to visit his family in Malaysia. So there we were—my husband, our three-year-old son and I, sitting across the aisle from my in-laws and our five-year-old nephew.

In 12 hours, we would be up to our eyeballs in tropical paradise—velvety sand beaches and endless emerald sea. But at that very moment on the airplane, I clutched the seat's armrests with sweaty palms. I wanted to turn the plane around.

It can't end this way, I thought, placing my palm on Xavier's chubby leg. He looked up at me and grinned then excitedly kicked the seat in front of us. Sudhagar, my husband—my pillar of strength, my rock—put his hand on mine and I smiled tightly.

Normally, I'm not a squeamish flier. Actually, I love the roller-coaster thrill of takeoff or landing. But this was nuts. I desperately searched the seat pocket for an airsickness bag and started mentally whipping out, "Hail Marys" and "Our Fathers."

I glanced across the aisle to see Amah, my Indian mother-in-law, praying to her Hindu gods, and Ayah, my father-in-law, sitting stone-faced. That's when my nephew, Darshana, started screaming in horror, causing Xavier to squeal in delight. Then Darshana yelled something in Telegu, the Indian dialect Sudhagar's family speaks. I don't understand Telegu, but I did understand the universal language of panic.

Later, I received the translation: "The plane is going down! The plane is going down! We are all going to die! We are all going to die!" I'm pretty sure everyone on the plane understood what he meant, too, even though they probably didn't speak Telegu, either.

"This is your captain speaking," a pleasant voice came over the intercom. Ayah clamped a hand over Darshana's mouth while Amah scolded. Scolding is another universal language I can understand. I have no idea what her words were, but I imagined it was along the lines of, "Stop saying that! We are not. Hey! Shut up before I throw you out of this plane!"

The captain continued, "For the next 20 minutes, we'll be going through a bit of turbulence."

A bit? More praying . . . must pray more.

"Please remain seated until I turn off the fasten-seat-belt sign. Thank you."

I glanced around the plane to see other passengers' reactions.

Some, like me, rapidly mouthed prayers. Others white-knuckled the armrests, pushed themselves back in their seats and squeezed their eyes shut.

The wind pitched us up then dropped us. My stomach jumped into my throat. I clamped my eyes shut and prayed harder. *I will not panic. I will not cry. I will keep it together.*

That's when my little Xavier squealed "Wheeeeeeeeee! Mommy, this is fun!"

I chuckled nervously, and a wave of laughter rippled throughout the small aircraft. Darshana, who, thank God, had stopped screaming, managed a laugh, too. Even though the turbulence remained and the landing left my knees shaky, we all handled the ride much better with that little burst of optimism from Xavier.

The next day at sunset, we ate a family dinner on Jimbaran Beach. As we waited for our seafood and tropical drinks, I walked with the kids down to the water's edge. The waves lapped at our toes, and I noticed two tiny containers constructed of palm leaves that held offerings of freshly picked flowers for the gods. A single stick of incense, stuck in the sand, stood sentinel between the two tiny shrines as the sun sunk into the water.

This was totally worth those 20 minutes of hell.

Now that I'm back in America, I can see that terrible flight as a metaphor for motherhood. You do, occasionally, hit turbulence. Sometimes you have to white-knuckle it and hold on tight. Other times, you scream—or cry, threaten, reason, beg, bargain or plead. If you're lucky, you have a husband who can be your calm in the storm or a little one who can provide some comic relief. When all else fails, just pray. Hunker down through the terrible turbulence, dream of white sand beaches and tropical waters. Hopefully, you'll earn your reward for a job well done on the exhilarating—and, at times, terrifying—ride called motherhood.

The Subramaniam family visited Bali in 2011.
From left to right: Amah, Ayah, Xavier, Darshana, Camille, and Sudhagar.

Open-Minded Mom

by
Pat Wahler

I always planned to be an open-minded mom, unlike my own parents who always said "No" to me faster than a hummingbird can flap its wings. So on the day my 11-year-old son Justin approached me with a request, I kept my mouth shut and let him talk.

"Mom, I want to get a snake."

After that, I couldn't have spoken if I had wanted to. Justin took my silence for agreeable interest and continued his pitch.

"The snake I want is a reticulated python. They're the biggest snakes in the world!"

My throat grew dry as he went on to inform me that snakes make interesting pets and that he'd learn a lot by having one. I couldn't help but admire his strategy. Clearly, he'd been planning his approach for a while. Finally, he delivered the coup de grâce.

"I already talked to Dad. He thinks it's a great idea."

While Justin waited for an answer, eyes wide with anticipation, I made a mental note to speak later to my traitorous husband, Phil. I couldn't bring myself to deflate Justin and searched for another way out. When our family rule about living within a budget came to mind, the words tumbled out.

"What does it cost to have a snake?"

After he had explained that the snake, glass habitat and other equipment would be about $250, I felt instant relief. Justin didn't have a dime that I knew about. By the time he could save such a sum, he'd certainly have moved on to another interest.

My jaw relaxed. I could afford to be open-minded now. "OK, here's the deal. If you can save the money and take full charge of its care, you can get a snake."

His face lit up like a sparkler on Fourth of July. "Thanks, Mom!"

My twinge of guilt didn't keep me from congratulating myself. I'd neatly side-stepped the role of party-pooper parent. Maybe in a few months we could talk about a more traditional pet for him. That thought eased my conscience enough to forget about the entire incident.

Months went by with no further mention of a snake until the day Justin burst through the front door, voice cracking with excitement.

"I saved the money!"

I didn't need to ask what he meant, as the horrifying details of our agreement flooded back. He'd mowed dozens of lawns over the summer. *Terrific*, I thought. *The neighbors get great-looking yards, and I get a snake. My parents were right. Maybe it's better to just say no.*

Though I'd have preferred getting a root canal, I drove

Justin to our local pet shop. He purchased everything he need-ed, including a young reticulated python. The snake was about 18 inches long with a striking gold, brown and black pattern. Its unblinking reptile eyes gave me shivers. I had no intention of getting cozy with our newest family member and declined when Justin offered to let me hold his new acquisition. All the way home, he talked about his plans for the newly christened friend he named "Monty Python."

Justin studied books on reptiles and practiced what he learned. He even kept a heavy rock on the habitat lid for extra security. I felt pleased enough about his sense of responsibility to dream about a future where Monty would become a science fair blue-ribbon winner.

Every few days, snakes must eat. By the time Monty was 3 feet long, his meals had evolved from mice to rats. Even though I acted as transport officer rather than executioner, I did not enjoy the process of delivering Monty's next victim. I began to wonder what might come next in his progressively growing food chain.

But other things soon distracted me. My job became more demanding than usual. I trudged home each evening with no energy to spare for worry. At the end of one particularly gruel-ing day, I crawled into bed and fell asleep as soon as my head touched the pillow.

Later than night, I woke to a semiconscious state. Some-thing heavy was on my foot. I pushed out my leg, rolled over and drifted back into dreams. Then a nagging awareness came again. Something moved against my ankle. *It has to be Phil playing one of his less-than-hilarious pranks.* Irritated and still half-asleep, I sat up, ready to let my husband have it.

In the light of the moon, I noticed the shadowy outline of something long and rope-like. The top of the shadow was nearly even with my face. I blinked and squinted. Monty came into focus with his body poised upright like a cobra ready to strike. My eyes jolted wide-open.

In one split second, I leapt to the floor and stumbled toward the light switch. I heard the sound of a piercing screech and realized it came from me. Even after blessed brightness flooded the room, I couldn't stop screaming like the heroine from a B-rated horror film.

Phil arrived on the scene first, interrupted from a late-night television program. Justin followed behind him, looking tousled and nearly as frantic as I did.

"I forgot to put the rock on the habitat. I'm sorry, Mom."

Justin scooped up the escapee, and both of them mercifully disappeared from view. Only Phil remained. His lips twitched, and his face reddened. He sputtered, coughed then started to laugh. I sat down hard, tears streaking my face.

"It's not funny, you know."

"I know."

He gasped out the words between guffaws. I gathered myself enough to get up and stalk away, checking the bed before I climbed back in. The lights remained on.

The next morning, I banished Monty to the basement. I couldn't get him far enough away from me, and no one dared argue the point. Despite Monty's relocation, nighttime still spooked me. No doubt I had contracted a severe case of PTSD . . . Post Traumatic Snake Disorder.

A few months later, my misery ended when Justin came to me in tears. Monty had passed away. Apparently a basement is not the best environment for a snake. I consoled Justin while artfully hiding my relief. Finally, I could put the whole experience—along with Monty—to rest. I slept better that night than I'd been able to for a long time.

But kids don't let moms forget.

Through the years, the story of my surprise visit from Monty became legend, resurrected at every family gathering. The constant reminders of that creepy-crawly night still haunted me. Yet I smiled along with everyone else, while silently cursing myself for ever letting a snake move in—until the day came when a grown-up Justin added a new element to the often-told story.

"Mom, my friends could never believe you actually let me have a snake. Thanks for being so understanding."

His words were sincere enough to soothe the soul of any open-minded mom. Perhaps I'd done the right thing after all. Taking a chance may have put a snake in my bed, but it also created an unforgettable memory, tacked into our life scrapbook with the glue of abundant love.

These days I'm looking forward rather than back. I plan to become known as an open-minded grandma, too.

With the right incentive, kids *can* save money, as Justin proved!

The Tooth Fairy's Bad Rep

by
Mary Horner

The tooth fairy has a bad reputation at my house, and with good reason—four of them, to be exact. Allow me to explain.

Reason #1: Her backstory is fuzzy

"Would you copy these words on a piece of paper for me?" my daughter asked one evening. "The words are 'hair,' 'love' and 'see you soon.'"

I did it without questioning.

"Thanks," she said and raced up to her room.

Later, she returned looking as if she had lost her best friend.

"What's the matter?" I asked.

"I'm trying to figure out if it was you or Daddy who actually wrote the note from the tooth fairy."

Uh-oh, I thought. "Really, and what did you find out?"

"It wasn't either one of you."

Thank God, my fake handwriting worked.

My daughter didn't realize it, but I was about to crack under the pressure. I was worried she would find out about the real tooth fairy, so I tried to keep from offering information I may have to defend or retract later.

This is one aspect of parenting no one discusses. We know about Santa, where he lives, what he does all year. But the tooth fairy? She is one elusive imp.

My kids kept asking me questions about the tooth fairy, and I couldn't answer them. We had read stories about her, but none seemed to satisfy their appetite for fairy knowledge.

I needed a guide to the tooth fairy that would tell me why she collected teeth and what she did with them. On several trips to the library, the kids and I found books I hoped would satisfy my kids' curiosity. One book said everything in Tooth Fairy Land was made out of teeth, including houses and roads.

"Where is Tooth Fairy Land?" my son asked, even though he was too young, at age four, to lose teeth.

"Uh, it's far, far away on the other side of the world."

My kids ran upstairs, where I was convinced they would discuss my answer. I felt smug. The other side of the world is a big place.

They ran back downstairs with a globe.

"You mean Tooth Fairy Land is in the Middle East?"

"Not exactly."

"The tooth fairy isn't in the war, is she?"

"No," I said. "You don't have to worry about that."

"What nationality is she?"

I told them she belonged to all the children in the world, and that her home isn't really on a map.

"Where is it, then? On the moon?"

"No, she doesn't live on the moon."

"Jupiter?"

"No."

"Mars? Is she a Martian tooth fairy? Cool."

"No, the tooth fairy is not a Martian."

I was trying to think fast, but nothing came to me.

"Then where does she live?"

I cracked under the pressure and said the first nondescript place I could think of.

"Underground."

"Like a mole? Does she have tunnels? How does she stay clean? Can she use her wand as a shovel to dig the tunnels? What does she do if she runs into an anthill?"

This was all happening too fast. I hadn't had my second cup of coffee yet. I was backed into such a tight corner that I considered telling the truth. I didn't want word getting out that the tooth fairy and yard rodents lived together underground. That could create all kinds of problems, especially when someone wanted to dig up the backyard for a pool or major landscaping.

"Actually," I said, thinking fast, "did I say underground? She used to live underground when I was a kid, but she moved. Her current address is on a cloud."

"Which one?"

"I don't know."

"Can we go out in the yard and look for her in the clouds?"

"Sure you can," I said. "If you see her, tell her I said hello!"

Reason #2: She doesn't see well in the dark

One morning, just as I was enjoying the act of rolling over and going back to sleep under the warmth of my comforter, my mind wandered a little too far into reality.

"Oh, damn!" I realized I had forgotten to attend to my duty as the person to collect the teeth and leave the money.

I jumped out of bed and found a couple of one-dollar bills in my dresser. I sneaked quietly into my son's room with the precise execution of a military maneuver. I crawled across the floor with the bills in my mouth so I wouldn't be seen if he accidentally woke up. He had slept on the far side of his bed by the window, so I didn't have to disturb him as I put the money under the part of the pillow closest to me. I held my breath and crawled back the way I had come in. I headed back to my room with his tooth, feeling self-satisfied. *I guess I'm not as bad at this as I thought,* I said to myself as I walked down the hall.

Later, one smiling boy with two bills in his hand woke me.

"Mom! Mom!" he shouted. "The tooth fairy gave me $21!"

"Oh, no," I said, realizing I'd given him my lunch money for the week.

"Why'd you say 'Oh, no'?" he asked.

"I meant to say "Oh, wow!"

"That's what I said, too. Oh, wow!"

#3: Her banking skills are subpar

When my daughter was about at the end of her tooth-losing days, anticipating a visit from the tooth fairy pulled her in opposite directions. The first was toward that magical land of childhood that filled the imagination with hopes and dreams and fairies and sparkles. The other was "too cool to care." In this case, "too cool to care" won out. And as much as I hated to see her grow up, I, feeling like the worst mother in the world, needed the cash.

By the time she lost the last baby tooth, she was "too cool to care" and didn't check under her pillow for several days after. Because it was her last baby tooth, and I was too lazy to break a $10 bill, I gave her more than I thought reasonable. Ten dollars was a tidy little sum for someone whose own tooth fairy had left her quarters and dimes back in the 1960s.

Unfortunately, my daughter never got the $10; she didn't check under her pillow. The Girl Scout from down the street delivered the cookies we had ordered six weeks earlier, and I was $3 short. I really did check my purse and the car for money, but I didn't have it. Just when I was about to pull up the couch cushions, I remembered the money under her pillow.

I ran upstairs and grabbed the $10, thinking I would replace it when I went to the bank. I replaced $7, which was the change I received from the Girl Scout.

The next day, my daughter still hadn't checked. I owed the piano teacher $2 more than my husband had in his wallet. I went upstairs during my daughter's lesson and reached under the pillow, pulling out $2.

I want to say I went to the bank and replaced the money.

But, I can't. What really happened was that night, my daughter checked under her pillow and found $5. And I felt a little guilty. However, she did eat a lot of Girl Scout cookies and benefited from the knowledge she gained from her piano lessons. So, I think the universe is OK with that. I know I am.

#4: The tooth fairy is forgetful

I promised myself I wouldn't forget to exchange the tooth for money when my son's next tooth fell out. I would be diligent and efficient, like the other moms. But a week later when he lost a tooth and told me he had carefully placed it under his pillow, I forgot.

Now, in my own defense, he stays up late and sometimes I fall asleep waiting for him to fall asleep. And did I tell you my son didn't sleep through the night until he was five? Seriously. Five years of sleep deprivation does weird things to a mother, like making her forget to do stuff people tell her to do. Please don't judge.

So the next morning, he came into my bedroom with the tooth.

"She didn't come," he said. "She forgot me."

My heart sank.

"Oh, honey," I said. "Did you look around really well and shake out the pillowcases in case she put it in one by mistake?"

Lucky me. Turns out he had done nothing more than run his hand under the pillow.

"Why don't you go get ready for school, and I'll take a look."

He agreed, reluctantly. As soon as he closed the door to

the bathroom, I flew down the hall to his room and put money inside the pillowcase. My heart was beating so hard I could feel it in my chest. I ran downstairs to load up his backpack for school and to pour some cereal into a bowl.

"Can I go look again?" he asked after he had eaten. "I didn't look inside the pillowcase."

"OK, since you're ready for school, you can go look."

Less than a minute later, he hurried back down the stairs.

"Hey, it was in the pillowcase."

"Well, what do you know?"

"Gotta go. The bus is coming."

He ran out the door on his way to the bus stop at the end of the driveway, looked up at the clouds in the sky and yelled, "Thank you!"

Buen Provecho!

by
Mary-Lane Kamberg

My daughter Johanna and I finished our Big Macs and dumped our trays of empty soft drink cups and hamburger wrappers into the trash.

"Remember, tomorrow's the fifth-grade 'Christmas Around the World feast,'" she said to me.

"Oh, yeah," I replied, hoping she didn't notice I'd forgotten. "What is it you're supposed to bring?"

"Anything from Spain," Johanna said.

"Any ideas?" I asked. Did the teacher expect me to be an international chef? The last foreign food I'd fixed was Italian spaghetti with old-world-style sauce that came in a jar. Then I remembered a recipe I could follow. "I'll make Spanish rice!"

"Ashley's already bringing that."

"You mean more than one kid chose Spain?"

Johanna nodded.

"How about tacos?" I asked.

"That's Mexico. Brett has Mexico."

"Is it too late to change countries?" I asked as we got into the car. "If you take China, we can order crab Rangoon at the Golden Bowl drive-thru. No, wait! France! You can take french fries!" I turned to go back into the restaurant.

Johanna glared. "It has to be from Spain."

"No problem," I said, forcing a smile, determined not to shirk this important mom duty. "We'll look in my cookbooks."

At home, Johanna perched on the end of my bed while I rummaged through the linen closet and found an armload of cookbooks I'd received as gifts from my well-meaning mother and sisters. "There's bound to be something in one of these," I said, spreading them across the bed as if I were dealing poker.

I picked up one at random. Johanna looked over my shoulder as I checked the index and found "Spanish bluebells." The corresponding page showed only a flower arrangement with sprigs of blue on a dining-room table. I flipped back to the index and found "Spanish moss." That picture showed a man sprinkling something onto a flowerbed.

Johanna grabbed the book and checked the cover. "This is a gardening book!"

The actual cookbooks in the pile were not helpful either. They listed only Spanish rice. My high-school-aged daughter Becky peeked into the room. "What are you guys doing?" she asked.

"Hey, maybe you can help," I said, motioning her inside. "Did you study anything about the cuisine in Spain in your Spanish class? We need a food from Spain."

Becky shrugged and left the room.

I phoned my mother for a suggestion.

"Spanish rice," she said.

"Ashley's bringing it."

"How about gazpacho?"

"What's in it?" I asked. As she described the cold tomato soup with cucumbers and onions, I repeated the ingredients for Johanna.

"Yuck!" she said. "No one will eat it."

Next, I tried my sister.

"Spanish rice," she said.

"Ashley's bringing it."

"Buy a jar of Spanish olives."

"Are those the green olives or the black ones?" I asked.

Johanna shook her head.

"No olives," I told my sister.

Johanna's hopeful look had transformed into one of desperation.

"I'll try Aunt Amy," I said to my daughter, trying to make my voice sound reassuring.

"Amy, Johanna's class is having 'Christmas Around the World' tomorrow, and we need a food from Spain besides Spanish rice, gazpacho or Spanish olives," I told her.

She consulted her cookbooks. "Sevillian salad," Amy said. "It has rice, onion and red and green peppers."

Johanna scrunched her face.

"How about Spanish corn?" Amy said. "It's corn with chili powder and olive oil."

"Gross," I said without consulting Johanna.

"Hold on a minute," Amy said. "Jon went to Spain."

"Honey," she hollered to her husband. "When you went to Spain, what did you eat?"

She relayed his reply. "He ate at McDonald's."

At bedtime, we were out of ideas. I tucked Johanna in and told her I'd get something to school in time for the 11:30 A.M. feast.

"Nothing gross, Mom," she said.

I promised.

The next morning, I headed for the store looking for something with a Spanish flair. Instead, I found teriyaki, German potato salad and Swiss chocolate. *I wish Johanna had chosen Japan. Or Germany. Or Switzerland. Anywhere but Spain.*

I steered my cart around the store. Then I remembered the treat Johanna had taken on her special day in kindergarten. Her teacher said the children had loved it! I gathered the ingredients and picked up a carton of party dip.

At home, I arranged the food on a serving tray and covered it with aluminum foil. Then I searched Becky's room for her Spanish-English dictionary. Carefully, I lettered an index card in Spanish, added phonetic spelling for the teacher and taped the card to the foil. Then I rushed to school, with little time to spare.

In Johanna's classroom, I walked in like a footman presenting treasure to a queen. "Legumbres from Spain," I announced.

Johanna sighed and smiled.

Her teacher clasped her hands in delight. "Oh, I'll have to try one!"

I left before the feast began.

After school, Johanna brought home the empty tray.

"Did the kids like the legumbres?" I asked.

"They liked them," she said, grinning. "But they're just vegetables and dip."

"I know," I said, beaming. "They have vegetables in Spain. And now your mom is an international chef!"

Trip of a Lifetime

by
Lisa Tognola

I used to travel to exotic places, act spontaneously and take risks. These days, adventure is a hibachi dinner at Benihana, and an epic adventure is when the chef's trick shrimp-toss into his pocket drops down my blouse by mistake.

So when my husband, Chris, informed me that I'd have to drive our 16-year-old daughter Heather and her friends to summer camp in the Poconos by myself because he'd be on a Las Vegas business trip (an oxymoron if I ever heard one), I worried.

"You'll be fine. You can do this," he said.

"But I'll have to cross the border!" I cried.

"Into Pennsylvania, not Afghanistan."

"Still, I'll have to pump my own gas."

"It's OK. You can ask for help. They speak English in Pennsylvania."

I had grown accustomed to a quiet suburban life. I didn't enjoy leaving home anymore, especially to enter the wilderness where I might face dangerous wildlife like snakes, bears and suburban campers.

But I wanted to expand my comfort zone and show my kids that each time we face our fears, we gain strength, courage and confidence. So I piled the car with sleeping bags, suitcases and teenage-girl camping essentials—curling irons, laptop computers and lip gloss. Then I spent the next two and a half hours driving in the rain and nagging my daughter to turn down the rap music blasting from the radio.

We'd barely left New Jersey when I spotted an unusual highway sign with a dotted image that resembled the children's game Connect the Dots. The sign said, "Keep Min One Space Apart." A series of equally spaced elliptical white dots marked the center of the road in front of me. I sped over them, not sure what to make of the painted ovals. It looked like a giant game of Road Twister for bored travelers. I was waiting for the next signs to say, "Left Tire, Green; Right Fender, Red."

"Did you girls see that unusual highway sign?" I asked. "Girls!" I shouted. Heather grunted and turned down the radio for a while, which allowed me to remove my fingers from my ears and steer without using my knees. It also gave me the chance to listen in on their conversation.

"I hope my counselor isn't Sarah," friend Amelia said. "She talks in her sleep all night."

"I know," answered Mary. "Then she complains the next morning that we kept her up late chatting."

"Look at the river!" Amelia exclaimed. "It's so beauti—

ewww! Road kill!"

We looked across the divide to see a freshly struck deer on the side of the highway. Vultures circled above.

"AHHHHHH!" the girls screamed.

It was horrible. All we needed was a pack of hyenas feeding on a young gazelle to complete the *Animal Planet* nightmare.

I was equally traumatized, but tried to make the best of the situation by using the experience as a teaching moment. I lectured the girls at length about urban sprawl displacing deer from their natural environment. "And that's why we have to pay attention to our surroundings while driving," I said. "Right, girls?"

Nobody responded, so I glanced in the rearview mirror and noticed they had all donned headphones. I sighed and turned on the news.

We finally pulled up to camp—in a downpour. By the time I unloaded the car, my clothes were completely soaked. I gave my daughter a wet hug and raced home, eager for this adventure to end.

I strained to hear NPR at full volume over the rain as I daydreamed about full-serve gas pumps and one less person to do laundry for. I was trying to ignore the distracting dots when a police siren sounded behind me. I pulled over.

"Mam, can you turn down your radio?"

"Sorry, officer," I said, and did as he asked.

"Do you know why I pulled you over?"

"No, officer," I answered, holding back my real guess: *Wet T-shirt?*

"You were tailgating." He handed me a ticket. "Next time, keep a minimum of one space apart—that's what the white dots are for."

Lesson learned: When we face our fears, we gain strength, courage and confidence, and, in some cases, a moving violation.

Lauren, Heather and Skyler

Meanest Mother in the World

by
Jan Morrill

The phone rang. Drying my hands with a dishtowel, I rushed to answer it.

"Hi, Mom." Hearing my daughter utter those two words, I knew something was wrong.

"Andrea? Everything OK?"

"It's not a big deal. I just need your advice . . ."

She needs my advice, I thought. This wasn't always so. I smiled and remembered like it was yesterday.

Andrea was 12—that challenging "tween" time, no longer a little girl, yet still far from being a young woman. The weekday morning had started like most. Andrea, my son, Adam, and I had rushed around trying to beat the clock to make it to work and school on time. I'd raised my voice a time or two in the process. OK, I'd yelled, while my kids countered with whined attempts at negotiation. At last, we were out the door and in the car.

We dropped Adam off at his elementary school and were running 10 minutes behind schedule. We still had one more stop—Andrea's junior high—before I could finally head to the office.

I felt my blood pressure rise as I realized I would be late for work again. My heart beat faster with the thought of each item on the day's to-do list. As I imagined a line of people waiting for me outside my office door when I arrived 10 minutes late, Andrea spoke.

"Mom?" She zipped and unzipped her backpack, clearly uncomfortable about saying what was on her mind. "Remember that guy you met at the football game last week?"

"The one who played the saxophone?"

"Yes, that one." She zipped and unzipped faster now. "Anyway, uh, he asked me to go to the movies with him tomorrow after school. Can I go?"

My heart fluttered. My little girl had just asked about going on a date! Her childhood, newborn to 12, flashed before my eyes.

I hardly thought about my reply before answering, "No, you're not old enough." My mother's instinct told me to prepare for the retort I knew would come, and I clenched the steering wheel.

Her eyes widened. "But ALL of my other friends get to go out on dates!" she cried. Her pitch rose with each squealed word.

I breathed in deep, prepared for battle. "Andrea, you're only 12. Sorry, you're not old enough to go on a date." I must admit, I couldn't resist reciting the old cliché that made me cringe every time my mother used it on me. "Besides, if all your friends jumped off a bridge, would you?"

Silence followed.

"I can't believe you won't let me go!" she whined. "You're the meanest mother in the world!"

Her words slapped me and amused me at the same time. Not yet accustomed to the highs and lows of my angel-daughter turned hormonal teenager, her reaction stung me. On the other hand, I wasn't too old to remember feeling the same anger toward my own mother—that oh, so desperate longing to go out with a boy versus Mom's overprotectiveness. Part of me felt Andrea's label of "The Meanest Mother in the World" was a Scarlet Letter. Part of me believed it was a Badge of Honor. Still, my hurt feelings—and my determination not to let her talk to me like that—made me do something I later thought I'd regret forever.

I pulled the car off the expressway onto a frontage road, slammed on the brakes and turned to Andrea. "If you think you can find a better mother, get out! And good luck finding her!" *That'll scare her all right. She'll learn never to talk back to me like that again.*

Andrea shot me one of her signature dirty looks—upper left lip raised in a scowl, accompanied by a roll of the eyes. Then she got out of the car and slammed the door behind her.

I was stunned. But, heck—I sure wasn't going to be the first one to give in. *I'll show her!* I sped away, though I kept my eye on the rearview mirror, ready to stop, but not one second before I saw her run after the car.

She did run. In the opposite direction.

I couldn't believe it. *Is it possible I raised a daughter more stubborn than me?*

It was time for the silly game to end. I looked for a place to turn around and go back. But to my horror, I realized the frontage road was one way only. I couldn't turn around.

A flood of consequences roared through my mind. *What if a stranger offered her a ride? Whisked her away?* I imagined waiting by the phone to hear word of her rescue, while cursing myself for my foolishness and pride. Jamming the accelerator to the floor, I raced to get to the opposite road. A new, frightening thought came to mind with every pounding beat of my heart. *How many lives will be changed forever because of one stupid, hasty decision?*

Back on the freeway, I exceeded 90 miles per hour, speeding to the frontage road exit that would take me back to my daughter. Racing seconds that dragged by, I silently pleaded, *Please-be-there-please-be-there-please-be-there.*

As I approached where she'd gotten out of the car, I found her. Relief washed over me, and I was sorry for how frightened my poor little girl must have been. All would be forgiven, and we would hold each other in a warm, thankful embrace.

I pulled the car up to where she stood, longing to have her safely beside me again.

But my anticipatory smile faded as she stood motionless, arms crossed defiantly. She glared at me, lip curled in a pouty snarl. Finally, she opened the door, got in the car and slammed the door shut.

"You're still the meanest mother in the world."

As I listened to Andrea on the other end of the phone line, I thought about how the bittersweet years of wearing her label, "Meanest Mother in the World" had flown by. But when I heard her say, "I need your advice," all of the bitterness was gone and only sweetness remained.

Andrea and mom Jan

Mind Over Middle School

by
Amy Mullis

This school year, I'm twitching like a substitute teacher with a cold sore in sex-ed class.

You see, I have a middle-schooler. Now, the possibility I might confuse the toothpaste with his hair gel in the morning is a real danger—as if I needed another Fruit Loop in the morning mix. But at least I'm confident my hair would have fluoride protection.

Because he is certain that I have the IQ of a bran flake, my son gave me detailed instructions for the school year. So that no one will suspect him of having actual parents, I should not be the first in line to pick him up at the end of the day. It's much cooler to hide behind the dumpsters and tap out a secret Navajo code when he wanders past—unless he is walking with a friend, in which case I should stuff my mouth with old bread wrappers to help me resist the urge to call out his name. My assignment for this year is to write cunning notes excusing him from gym class.

This morning, in the time I usually reserve for scavenging for coffee money in the glove compartment, I found a small packet of curled papers, one folded intricately into a paper football. This highly official document, addressed to me personally (Parent or Guardian), bore the title, "Questionnaire from Teacher," and was obviously written for purposes of public humiliation. My son hasn't given me this much intimate information about himself since he could form the words "No comment" without spitting applesauce down his chin.

I opened the form and began to read: "Does he have any health problems?" (It depends. Is potty mouth a disease or strictly a condition treated by telephone restriction and the loss of electronic entertainment?) "What is the name and phone number of the nearest relative not living with you?" (My ex-husband. Thanks for the memories.)

Chuckling to myself, I fumbled in my purse for a pen. All I could find was a tube of travel-sized toothpaste and a Q-Tip. My choice of writing utensil would probably result in more questions, but at least the paper would have a clean, fresh taste.

Squinting through my bifocals and dipping my Q-Tip in Icy Mint Gel, I proceeded with answering the questions.

Question: Is your child organized?
Answer: Yes. He has 3,962 trading cards perfectly categorized in three-ring binders and labeled as to type, condition and year. Each one is logged in a notebook tagged with a se-

curity sensor that emits a deafening noise, lays down a toxic smoke screen and dials the emergency squad if disturbed by a younger brother. These notebooks are strategically hidden beneath 3 tons of toxic waste on his bedroom floor.

Question: How much time does your child spend on homework?
Answer: He has homework?

Question: What subject takes the most homework time?
Answer: He has different subjects?

Question: How would you rate your child's social skills?
Answer: This is difficult to answer. If, by social skills, you mean does he gargle green JELL-O at the dinner table or spit down his brother's shirt when there are no witnesses, I would say he reeks of social skills. Of course, the same child is likely to become invisible if I mention the word "underwear" in public.

Question: How can I best help your child learn?
Answer: Insert homework material into commercial segments that air during television shows offering Japanese animation. This kid memorized the words to every commercial made since 1987, but he cannot recall his address and date of birth unless a mail-in rebate is involved.

Question: What special facts do I need to know to help your child learn?
Answer: He considers it a personal insult to be included in vocabulary tests. He is offended by teachers with fussy hairdos or bizarre mannerisms (such as weeping bitterly at the beginning

of the school day). He prefers ice cream over meatloaf for lunch, loathes science projects and thinks teachers who wear pith helmets to school are neat.

Question: What are your child's goals for the year?
Answer: To sleep until 7:45 every morning, to exist for an entire year on curly fries and carbonated beverages and to wear cooler clothes than T. J., who sports a dog chain around his neck and torn boxer shorts over his pants.

Question: Whom do I call in case of emergency?
Answer: 911.

Honestly, you'd think a teacher would know that.

Mom Amy and son Ryan

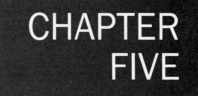

Day In
and Day Out

As moms, our work is never done.

Breakfast is for Champions and Chumps

by
Lucia Paul

How did I end up with 300 pounds of bananas in my car? I wish that question was the setup to a bad joke. But it's not. In the world of school volunteerism, beware these four words: "It's no big deal." You might also want to be cautious of "It's super easy" and "A complete no-brainer."

When I was approached to co-chair the four—yes, I said four—family breakfasts for my son's school, I didn't have a primer on what certain volunteer-luring catch phrases really meant. The one I fell for was, "We just set out a bunch of do-nuts and some coffee . . . sometimes there's cereal. But that's donated."

First, I should probably explain why there are four family breakfasts at our school—there is a breakfast for practically everyone. There are the mother-son and father-daughter breakfasts, which, of course, leads to the inevitable mother-daughter and father-son breakfasts. Yes, a no-brainer.

Now to the real meat—or banana—of the story.

Clearly, I agreed to the position of family breakfast co-chair. As the mom of children spaced seven years apart, I have traveled the crowded road of "Grade Mom," with a stop at "Call-Me-If-You-Get-Short-Handed Mom" to my final destination of "Wait—I-Have-Children? Mom." Agreeing to my new job was somewhere in the middle of that journey. Like any devious plot, it was only when the layers began to be gently peeled away (still on the banana theme) that the real situation was revealed.

The first layer was attending the meeting where my co-chair and I learned what was involved in creating the events. On four mornings—paired fall and spring over back-to-back days—we would serve breakfast before school each morning to between 350 and 500 parents, grandparents, family friends and students, as many as 1,000 meals in two days. At the meeting, we discovered that the breakfast included coffee, juice, milk, cereal, bananas, donuts and muffins.

Providing this food for two to 20 people is nothing. But when serving a huge crowd two days in a row, it's like an episode of *Homeland*. Picture my sainted co-chair Angela and I with a large corkboard covered with lists, schedules and notes. "Angela!" I say dramatically, pushing my hair back from my face. "You've got to start brewing coffee at 5:30 A.M. We'll never make it! The machine takes an hour just to heat! Just to heat!" I punch the wall and curse. If you're a fan of the show like me, you will appreciate the comparison.

Understand that the whole event undertaking was explained to us in the same offhand way you might say, "Could you hand me the salt?" At that fateful meeting, we learned what the family breakfast looked like on paper. The previous schedule went something like this:

Two weeks before: Purchase 2,000 hot/cold cups, 2,000 paper napkins, 3,000 coffee stirrers, 800 bowls, 800 spoons and 36 football fields worth of plastic table coverings. (I'm only kidding about the number of table coverings.)

One week before: Purchase 30 pounds of coffee, order 600 donuts per morning (one for each person plus a few extras), secure 20 donated coffee thermoses, remind volunteers of their arrival time, pre-order delivery of 40 gallons of milk and 40 gallons of orange juice, purchase 800 individual one-serving boxes of cereal (Someone had better like Raisin Bran, because it's always in the family pack twice).

Morning of the event: Be at school no later than 4:45 A.M. to preheat the commercial coffee maker, arrange 40 carnations into small bouquets, which no one will care about, and find the aprons with "Family Breakfast" embroidered on them. There will be four aprons and 15 volunteers. Prepare to be asked if there is decaf and tea. There is not. There is also no skim milk or fresh fruit, and there are no lattes.

My own family members were blind to my burden and expected their breakfast to be laid out before I backed out of the driveway at dawn. I supplied granola bars and a small salute.

Which brings me all the way back to the 300 pounds of bananas. The day before the event, Angela and I remembered we had foolishly advertised to the general population that there would be bananas at the breakfasts: "Come share a doughnut, juice, cereal, coffee and a banana with someone you love at Family Breakfast!" We'd promised bananas, and, by God, there would be bananas!

We figured that not all attendees would actually eat a banana. Back to *Homeland*: "That's 400 to 600 bananas on the low end," I said, pacing back and forth while gesturing wildly at the corkboard. "How do we do it?" I grab Angela by the lapels. (She does wear collared shirts sometimes.) "How in the name of all that is holy do we do it?"

It turned out we did it by me driving to Rainbow Foods in my Grand Cherokee and loading the passenger, back and cargo seats with bananas. There were more than 300 pounds. I know because they charge by the pound. I have never spent time on a banana plantation, but I now have a fair idea of what one smells like.

Family Breakfast is like a wedding—there's a lot of planning and preparation before the day arrives. Then it's over in a blur. Our blur looked like children from *The Hunger Games* seeking donuts.

"They have donuts every day of the week at Super America!" I shouted to no avail. Apparently, I am in a minority of moms who dole out donuts pretty regularly instead of like caviar from the Caspian Sea.

It all worked out: adults had coffee; children had donuts. But in the craziness, I had neglected to realize one thing—this was a two-year volunteer commitment. Angela and I would be back at it again next year.

Can you guess which edible item would be missing from the list next time? Here's a hint: It's yellow, and you can fit a surprising number of them in your car.

Lucia and a few of her bananas

Balancing Act

by
Rebecca MacKenzie

I'd planned to return to work after the birth of our daughter Elyssa, and the time to surrender her care was approaching too fast. My husband, Ken, and I made a confirmation call to our prospective child-care provider.

"Hi, Susan. I'm checking to make sure we're good to go for the 27th."

"Yes, we are," she replied. Suddenly, she said, "Whoops! Oh, no! Can you hold on a minute?"

Sounds of dogs barking and kids yelling and metal clattering and general chaos made their way over the phone line and into my anxious ear. I flinched when I heard, "Fire!"

Susan came back on the line, breathless. "Can I call you back? We have a little emergency." Her tone was agitated and her words, rushed.

"Sure," I responded, but Susan had already hung up.

I related what I had heard, but Ken did not need my sum-mation. The look on my face was sufficient to immediately alter our plans. We spontaneously and adamantly decided I would not return to my job and that I would become a stay-at-home mom.

Some of the personal ramifications of this decision I had anticipated—the loss of income, the lack of adult interaction and even the erratic schedule. However, the bitterness and re-sentment I felt toward my husband caught me by surprise.

Each day, Ken left for work, returned from work, took his evening walk, did his exercises, indulged in a shower and read his newspaper while waiting for his supper to be set in front of him. His life-after-childbirth had not changed at all. My post-baby life, however, had done a 180.

We sold my new car because we no longer had my income to cover the payments. Since Ken needed to use our remaining vehicle to get to his job, I was housebound. Without a car to drive to the grocery store or to run other errands, I truly was a STAY-at-home mom!

Being jobless equated to no high-priority projects and no resulting sense of accomplishment, no monetary compensation and no high status or professional advancement. There were no rushed lunches with co-workers or water-cooler conversations talking about the previous night's television viewing. There no longer was any need to dress professionally—no choosing the right outfit for the day and accessorizing it perfectly. Instead, I was seldom out of my pajamas before lunchtime, and I usually didn't get a shower until midday when Elyssa napped.

I was jealous of Ken's life outside our home. My envy

eroded my self-worth and ate away at my self-image until I became a witch with a capital "B."

After 10 months of staying home with Elyssa, I lambasted my husband at full volume. "Your life has not changed one iota, while MY life has done an about-face!"

"I don't understand what you're upset about. Didn't you want to stay home?"

"No, I didn't 'want' to stay home. WE agreed it was necessary. I'm used to being compensated for the work I do. There's not even a sense of appreciation here!"

"I'm not going to 'pay' you for breathing!"

Shocked, I realized that Ken had no concept of homemaking and child rearing as work. He held the archaic belief that because I was female, these things were as natural as breathing.

Deciding it was time Ken got a taste of stay-at-home parenting, I planned an overnight visit to my aunt's house. Thank goodness my sister agreed to accompany me—since we had sold my car, using her car was the only way I could escape.

I enjoyed my sister's company and the hour's ride to our destination. It was pleasant to travel even this short distance. My aunt made a marvelous dinner for us, and her home was comfortable and quiet. I didn't have to cook, clean, change diapers or tend to a baby's cries. I pampered myself with a long, hot shower that night and slept later than usual in the morning.

The second day seemed long, though. We went to the mall, and I found myself wandering to the kids' section of every department store we visited. My conversation started to fixate on Elyssa and Ken. Finally, after dinner, it was time to drive home, and I was eager to be there.

I began to wonder what I would find upon my return. *Will Ken have Elyssa bathed and tucked in for the night? Will he be glad to see me, perhaps have a bottle of wine chilling? Will he appreciate me now?*

Hoping to find our daughter sound asleep and my husband eagerly awaiting my return, I instead found Ken hosting a party in our well-lit backyard! Many of our friends were there, enjoying grilled burgers and cold drinks.

Well past her bedtime, Elyssa sat on the patio with a piece of chocolate cake on a paper plate between her chubby legs. Judging by her frosting-covered smile and cake-mittened hands, she had enjoyed the dessert essentially unsupervised.

Ken was glad to see me and welcomed me with an enthusiastic kiss. I suspected part of that enthusiasm was because now I could put Elyssa to bed for him.

My jaunt had done little to educate my husband on the domestic demands of a stay-at-home parent. Ironically, because the overnight visit had energized me, it was I who learned a valuable lesson—keeping myself refreshed and my life well-balanced are two keys to domestic success.

I also learned that a grilled burger and some chocolate cake can contribute significantly to that balance.

Mom in the Middle

by
Dacia Wilkinson

There are days when I believe I should simply stand in the middle of the living room with arms outstretched as my family moves around me, talking to me, wanting my attention, needing something fixed or kissed or hugged or found. Trying to accomplish my own goals seems selfish in the midst of the flurry of seven other people who all share my last name and six of them, my DNA. They're everywhere.

And sometimes, I just want to breathe.

For three and a half years, I have clung to my time in the classroom at the college where I teach, enjoying who I am in that environment, needing that rush that comes from watching light bulbs go off in eyes when my adult students hear something that changes their thought processes concerning their future. People take notes and ask questions. They raise their hands. I'm on fire. That is air I can breathe.

A few weeks ago, two young adult women in my classroom began to scream at each other. One had arrived an hour late. After handing her the paper, I told her what to do on the midterm. Her neighbor told her what to do on the midterm. A girl from the second row turned around and told her what to do on the midterm. The late girl snapped, coming to her feet with an accompanying jerk of her head and flick of her wrist in an "I'm grown" gesture. Apparently, she felt the third time was too much.

Screaming erupted between late girl and second-row girl—expletives flew, drawing shock from the faces of students sitting nearby. My head reeled, déjà vu set in, and with a sound, stinging clap of my hands and a stern, "Stop it!" I gained control of the situation by moving to stand in the middle. Just like home. Just as if it were my teenage daughters. I'm a mom—always—and though I might try to escape it for a few hours a week, I can't. It's who I am. It's how I breathe.

I upset one of my little men earlier this evening because he didn't want tacos for dinner. The crying that ensued could have woken a few dead—I apologize if there were zombies in your neighborhood, on the front porch, climbing over the wood fence in the backyard and trampling plants and shrubbery.

He was loud, and so to bed he went. Another little man decided he had been punished, too—why, I have no idea—and his crying echoed his older brother's.

Whatever, I said to myself. "You're in bed, too," I said to #2.

A dramatic and emotional hour later, both were asleep in separate rooms. I stood in the middle to watch my sweet little angel boys, and turned my head back and forth. I caught my breath.

I'm a mom in the middle, living in two worlds—eternally the mom in both, taking one day at a time, and remembering to breathe.

Across the back, L to R:. Husband Kyle, Dacia, Kennedy, and Keenan. Front, L to R: Koel and Kadi, Klayton, and Koby Kidd

Mama Loca

by
Pat Nelson

I'll admit it—at times, I was a harried mom. Crazy. Loca. I've never trusted any mom who says she is always cool, calm and collected because sometimes, there are moments of loca in everyone.

My little Susan was such a sweetheart, always smiling. She didn't talk much until she was past two years of age. That's when I finally got to spend time alone with her while my four-year-old son, Steven, was in preschool. I held Susan's tiny hand as we walked the downtown sidewalks together, and we chattered about the things we saw in the stores or in the sky or at our feet. Susan became talkative, which was a bit unusual, since normally she was a quiet child. I wondered if maybe she hadn't talked much before because I was so busy pointing out absolutely everything that would introduce my baby girl to the world. Or maybe it was because her brother, Steven, usually did her talking for her. But I was happy she had finally found her voice.

I worked part-time at a credit union, so days off were full of errands. One day, I had to visit the repair shop to buy a part for the car. I stood at the service window, the smell of automotive grease permeating my coat and my hair and becoming my perfume. I had a million things on my list, and I wanted to finish half of them before Steven got out of preschool. I had only two hours, and I was at full speed. The man at the service desk was in no hurry. He took another swig from a well-used coffee cup before ambling up to the window.

Come on, Mister, I have things to do and places to be! Hurry up! Ándale! I quietly fumed.

"What can I do for you?" he asked, not looking very motivated to do anything.

Suddenly, I snapped. Susan was standing next to me, but my son had run off somewhere. "Steven, Steven, where are you? Hang on. I have to find my son." *How could Steven do this to me when I'm in such a hurry? Grrr!*

Confused, I thought Steven was with us, as well. With enough volume for everyone in the whole place to hear, Susan hollered, "Mommy, we took Steven to school!"

When I shouted for him again, my daughter repeated, "Mommy, remember? We just took Steven to school!"

In my agitation, words from my limited Spanish vocabulary flew out of my mouth: *"¡Ay, caramba!"* Why hadn't I been happy to allow her to remain a quiet little girl who seldom spoke? I hurried with my business at the repair shop and got the heck out of there. It was my turn to *ándale!*

When Susan was five, she started kindergarten. Steven, in

second grade, rode the bus to school. I was working full time by then, but had a day off. My list of errands was long. I drove Susan to kindergarten, thinking as I drove down the hill about each stop I would make once I had deposited her at school.

The more errands I thought of, the faster I drove down the curvy road. *Ándale! Ándale!* By the time I had reached the bottom of the hill—just before the 15-mph school zone— I was going 55! I immediately forgot about my list of tasks once I noticed the red flashing lights behind me. As upset as I was about getting a ticket, I was relieved that the officer had stopped me a few feet before I reached the school zone, where the ticket amount would have quickly multiplied.

The officer approached my driver's-side window and looked at my daughter. "How are you, young fella?" he asked. She hung her head, embarrassed that he had thought she was a boy.

Then he looked at me and sternly warned, "You need to slow down and keep that little one of yours safe."

I agreed then offered to let my daughter walk across the crosswalk to go to school while I continued to receive from the officer the lecture I deserved.

While the officer shamed me and wrote my ticket, my daughter walked down the street and crossed by herself for the first time ever at the crosswalk that led to the school. She was proud. But in the car, I was ashamed of myself for being in such a hurry.

Now, thinking back, I have to wonder if some of the craziest moments could have been avoided if I had just slowed down. But how? My kids are now grown and my grandkids are nearly grown. And the list of errands still makes me tell myself *ándale, ándale* . . . and it still sometimes makes me feel like a loca mama.

Susan and Steven

Where Did I Go Wrong?

by
Eva Lesko Natiello

Whether or not you suffer from chronic parenting inse-curity, odds are it's probably crept up at some point. It's that thorny feeling of self-doubt when you can't seem to come up with the right thing to say or do when mature, thoughtful ac-tion is required. And sometimes, insecurity rears its ugly head in the form of jealousy toward another mom who just seems to do momhood better than you.

I was sitting at my son's first basketball practice with a new team. The gym was too far from our house to drop him off, so I sat there for the duration. The practice ran from 5:30 to 7 o'clock—a bummer of a time slot.

I turned to one of the moms on the bleachers and said, "If only I could figure out how to get dinner done while I'm sitting here."

She laughed. "Yeah. Let me know if you figure that out."

A moment later, she got a text from her daughter. She turned to me and said, "Looks like I figured it out. I've got my 21-year-old daughter on it."

"That's awesome," I said.

"When you have six, they all have to help out."

Six! Geez, I thought. I didn't know anyone with six kids. But I was even more impressed that they all helped out.

That's where I had gone wrong—I only had two kids, and while they're not slackers, I hadn't given them tons of responsibility. I should've been doling out age-appropriate chores early on so it would have become part of the fabric of our lives, as this woman sitting next to me had done. At that moment, I wasn't feeling very good about my parenting. *All that lost time. My kids aren't prepared for the real world.*

Right then I made a quick decision—more chores! Then I thought about my kids' schedules. They're far busier than I ever was at their age. I was 10 when I was sent to the grocery for milk or eggs. I was doing the laundry when I was 13. But nowadays, kids are being groomed to become competitive soccer players, professional singers and actors and straight-A students. They are immersed in special coaching, training, tutors, classes and teams, which is another discussion altogether. They don't have time to clean out the garage and cut the grass—instead, they need personal assistants. Guess who gets that job?

"Wow, how do you do it with six kids?" I asked. I was officially captivated.

"Well, since I work full time, I really can't do it unless the kids do their share."

Full time! I looked at this mom with wonder. It's possible my jaw dropped. She was amazing. And in control. She was doing her thing while empowering her kids with life skills. They were learning how to become self-reliant.

I shook my head. *Maybe it's not too late for me to turn things around with my kids.* This other mom's kids wouldn't be starving at college someday, wearing filthy clothes, waiting for a ride to Poli Sci—that's for sure. I envied her. Her kids were so accustomed to doing things around their house they probably did the laundry without being asked. They probably noticed on their own when the hamper was full and stuck a load in to stave off a sockless morning. *Those kids are something.*

The mom's phone rang. Her daughter was calling with progress on dinner.

I tried to imagine what the daughter was preparing. I might've been hallucinating, but I actually smelled something cooking. I had a vision of their kitchen and the table was set, thanks to one of her younger kids.

The beep of a new text chirped.

"My daughter," she said with deserved pride.

My eyes grew as wide as dessert plates. I waited to hear more.

"She called Kentucky Fried Chicken. They have an eight-piece meal for $4.99." Then she dusted off her hands. "Dinner is done."

My daydreaming screeched to a stop. "Really?" I said. "That's a great deal."

"I know."

"And your daughter will have it on the table by the time

you get home."

She looked at me like I was nuts. "Who? That lazy thing?! I'll be lucky if she's out of her pajamas."

Mommy Wars

by
Kristen Capps

Living in a beautiful suburban house with a white picket fence seems like the American dream, but it has its challenges. Neighborhoods become Gossip Central, causing some women to take on a whole new attitude. I learned quickly that it's a dog-eat-dog world, and the competitiveness between women is fierce.

I loved being a stay-at-home mom, but when I entered the workforce, things changed drastically. I was no longer included in the mommy group, but was now considered an outsider, cut off the email list for group gatherings and monthly Bunko nights.

I lived in a cul-de-sac consisting of young families, and the women were all stay-at-home moms. Between Pampered Chef parties and scrapbooking, together we girls had become confidants and lifelong friends. We covered for each other. If there was a hair-pulling moment at home and one of our group was feeling overwhelmed, another would say, "Send the boys over and take some time to yourself." What a great group of women I called my friends. Sure, there were the occasional bouts of constructive gossip about each other, but overall, our group maintained a special bond. We were raising our children together, providing stable homes and keeping our husbands happy.

A year had passed; my babies were getting older and a teaching spot had opened up in the nearby school district. Teachers are only hired once a year, so I had to at least apply. I went to the interview, and lo and behold, I got the job! *Crap! Now what?* popped into my mind. *I wasn't expecting this!* I needed to talk to the ladies and get their support, so we all got together for our monthly Bunko game.

When I shared my news, my friends glared at me as if I had shared their most intimate secrets on my blog. *Wow, thanks for the support.* Instantly, I had become one of "those" moms. The working mom! Instead of leaving Bunko after the cold reception of my news of employment, I wallowed in three more glasses of wine and staggered home to pout about the unfortunate mess I had gotten myself into. I proceeded to slur out the news to my husband as well as my current buzz would allow.

"I can't believe they are mad at me. They think I am leaving my kids and my friends behind for money!"

I was swaying to and fro, pleading my displeasure to him. Standing in his boxers in our bedroom, he cut me off mid-sentence. With a mouth full of peanut butter crackers, he barked, "What do you care what they think?"

What is he saying? Between burps and head spins, I sobbed, "Of course, I care! They are my best friends ever! What am I going to do now?"

Unfortunately, in a more sober state, I later realized they

weren't really my friends, but now my judgmental neighbors. Life had taken a turn. The bond was broken, and I couldn't have become more of an outcast. I thought these things only happened on *Housewives of Wherever*. Thoughts ran through my mind: *Were my friends being childish? Were they jealous? Or was I being an unacceptable wife and mother by joining the workforce?*

Working full time was challenging. I couldn't find a matching pair of socks to save my life. And for the first time, the pee stains in the bathrooms I cleaned daily were not only visible—you could smell them, too. My children no longer had their lunches packed with cutesy "Love ya" notes inside. Hell, I was lucky if I remembered to pack their Capri Suns.

I had two in elementary school and two enrolled in the Montessori private school. Life was hectic but almost manageable. So I thought. Then came the day when I was up against the wall, questioning my motherhood and womanhood. My youngest son's teacher called and said my son had been coming to school without wearing any underwear. Because the stalls didn't have doors, the other children could see everything. I was mortified. My response was simply, "Well, he left *home* with his undies on." How stupid did that sound?

I might miss a snack or forget to sign a homework planner, but I know that my kids wear underwear! *What will the teachers think of me?* I worried. *That we can't afford underwear? Have I just failed as a mom in the skivvy department? What would my neighbors think if they found out? What would my own mom think?*

Come to find out, my son was taking them off in the car and hiding them in his school bag. He just didn't like to wear his shorts.

I shared the entire episode with my husband, who laughed his ass off. His delight caused me to become more insecure about what my women cohorts would say. Thinking about it caused a mortified flush to creep up my face.

The next reality check came one Saturday morning. Youth soccer was in full swing, and it was the playoff game for my son's team—the Centipedes. It was also my day to bring snacks, so I ran to the store for the standard 24-pack of Goldfish crackers. I was thrilled that I had remembered it was my snack day. But the pat on my back stopped short when I turned and saw Muriel—who shared that snack day with me—passing out individualized Ziploc baggies filled with a variety of fruit.

How the hell did she have time to do that? I asked myself.

When I thought I couldn't feel any more inadequate, she brought out a fancy tray of Rice Crispy treats. Shaped like soccer balls, each one had a player's name on it. The kids went wild for the awesome goodies, and Muriel smiled from ear to ear, as the boys ran by me and said, "Thanks, Mrs. Capps, for the Goldfish." I cringed inside at the thought of my measly snack crackers up against Muriel's extraordinary treats. I wasn't worried so much about what my kid thought of my snack—food is food. I was more troubled by what Muriel thought of me as a mom. *Competition over the best snack? Really? Who had I become?*

Time was mocking me. It refused to slow down so that I could do what I needed to do—work and maintain our household. I looked at myself in the mirror and cried. I'd gone from perky to matronly in such a short time. I hated to think of what I would look like in five years.

Finally, I had had enough. This was the call to arms, the time of self-preservation! I was going to do double-duty—I was going to take care of my job and my family. I ordered a Franklin Covey calendar and color-coded the kids' activities with separate highlighters for each. I did my lesson plans at school before I left and did the 10-second tidy each day.

Things looked good for about two weeks, and then the crows' feet became much more evident. *Damn, I'm tired.* The old saying, "Jack of all trades . . ." was fitting, but I wondered if Jack was as exhausted as I was. Who was I trying to impress, anyway? June Cleaver exemplified the American housewife and her family adored her. Gloria Steinem was a woman of power and an inspiration to others to move forward. Why couldn't I be a blend of both women without others throwing in their two cents?

I started hanging out with the women from work and reading *More* magazine in search of answers. When I realized I was not the only woman out there in search of work/life balance, I didn't feel so alone in my quest.

From that day on, I have busted ass to try to do it all. The vicious cycle of maintaining the household and keeping the family happy, while trying to do my job as a teacher and care for 100 high school kids each day, has become a difficult undertaking, but I've found it can be done.

I would be lying if I said I don't care what other people think, especially what other women think. Worrying about womanly perception is exhausting, but after enough worry and embarrassment, I've learned to care less. I realized that we all have preferences for our own lifestyles. It isn't that we compete as wives or mothers . . . we compete as women. We are all looking for recognition and acceptance by our peers. We really don't care that much how our children feel about getting Goldfish crackers instead of fancy snacks. After all, at the end of the day, they are lucky to get snacks at all.

Caring moms who stay at home work their butts off, and caring moms who work outside the home do the same. So really, we are all in the same boat. In the end, only one thing really matters—making sure your kids go to school wearing their underpants.

L to R: surrrounding Mom, is Josh (age 12), Dylan (16), Conner (14), and Hunter (18)

Extra Baggage

by
Kelly Melang

Today I officially entered the world of plumbers—no education or degrees involved. I accidentally showed my plumber's butt.

It started with a pair of low-rise jeans. I fought those jeans tooth and nail, because I have what's politely referred to as a "baby belly." No, I'm not pregnant. But I was, and after two children, my stomach doesn't hold the tautness of my youth. Gravity has created the pooch—the muffin top—the extra baggage that was once called "love handles." I've accepted my body for what it is, because I can't afford the amount of plastic surgery it would take to get the old one back.

I am not the best candidate for low-rise jeans. I don't want anything hanging over the sides of my pants. So, until now, I stayed with "granny jeans." Granny jeans sit comfortably (not!) at the middle of my waist. The zipper is long enough to have a ZIP code, and if I really want to be comfortable, then I can buy the ones with stretchy fabric. But recently my friend dared me to try a pair of low-rise jeans. Never take the dare of a friend who only has a one-child belly.

"You'll love them," she said. "They are so comfortable."

"But what about this skin hanging over?"

"What about it?"

"Oh, never mind."

I tried them on and was surprised. They are actually comfortable! Granny jeans do not give in the waist, and they pinch the extra skin I support in my middle. When I take them off, I have what looks like a botched C-section scar running across my stomach from the fabric pressing against my skin. With low-rise jeans, there isn't any fabric to dig into my waist.

I tried to find the zipper and located a tiny, half-inch, three-toothed thing. *Why even put a zipper on jeans if it's so small you can't find it?* I wondered. I forgot about moving into the moo moo stage of my life as I bought two pairs and decided to go with a fashion trend.

I wore my new jeans proudly, feeling a little sassy at the freedom I felt; that is, until I did something that took away my sassiness and flushed it right down the toilet. It's amazing how something so normal and innocent can become something sordid in a split second. I bent over to pick up one of my children, and immediately I entered the realm normally inhabited by men under a kitchen sink with pipes. I showed my flesh as the other mothers in my group gasped.

"What?" I stood up, and my sideways smile disappeared.

"You're showing mommy butt," one of them whispered.

"Mommy butt?"

"Yeah, it's plumber's butt, except on a mom."

My hand immediately flew to the back of my ultracomfortable low-rise jeans.

I didn't want to believe it. Had I sunk so low in worrying about the extra baggage around my middle that I didn't care about showing the extra baggage on my end? I thought about the time I watched a man expose more than I had ever hoped to see in my lifetime as he tried to fix a snowmobile on the ski slope. My horror had been quickly replaced by curiosity as I fought the urge to go ask him if he felt a draft back there.

The other moms explained to me that while low-rise jeans are comfortable, those of us with a midsection that hasn't seen the light of day since before our first child was born can't wear the shorter T-shirts without the risk of showing mommy butt. They took me back to the store and showed me the reason for the trend in longer shirts. Those shirts were meant to cover up what nature did not intend for little eyes to see—Mommy's extra belly skin that, when squished together, resembles a butt. I gleefully bought several shirts and decided to go with a second fashion trend, designed to (literally) cover up the first.

Now my lovely babydoll tops, paired with my low-rise jeans, are long enough to protect my assets while I hold onto the last vestiges of youth. I'd ask my husband if I look hot, but we all know his opinion is skewed; he's looking to get lucky. I'll take one more turn in the mirror then step out, confident in myself. I've had enough of trying to be something I'm not. I'll never be a plumber again.

Dusty Drawers

by
Linda Wolff

If you thought you heard someone scream, "Calgon, take me away!" you heard right.

Cleaning up messy spills, playing taxi driver, wiping little tushies, preparing sack lunches, helping with homework, giving bubble baths and reading bedtime stories is a 24/7 job. We can all agree a mom's work is never done.

Of course, the impromptu yummy hugs and sloppy kisses are sweet bliss, but I'd be lying if I didn't admit that being a mom is sometimes full of domestic drudgery. So forgive me if my mind wanders to greener and more pleasurable pastures where I don't have someone else's food on my shirt. In my daydreams, my life is exciting and unpredictable, I get to take long uninterrupted showers and my hair always looks good.

That's right, when my heavy head finally hits the pillow in those deliciously silent moments before I drift off into slumber, I begin to imagine the furthest thing from reality—that I'm a Bond Girl.

It's my survival mechanism. For example, while drifting off, I'll mentally review tomorrow's to-do list—which is far better than counting sheep—and pretend it's all for the good of a top-secret mission:

1) Pick up dry-cleaning, deflect questions as to why everything has chocolate and red wine stains;

2) Go to hardware store to replenish, yet again, enough paint and spackle to cover the hole the kids dug into the wall to create their secret cave;

3) Buy red grapes, firm, not squishy, or the youngest in power won't touch them and therefore will dash any chance of real fruit consumption.

And I do all of this, plus more, with nary a yoga pant or mom jean or hair scrunchie in sight. That's what Bond Girls do.

You see, I've been besotted by Sean Connery, Roger Moore, Pierce Brosnan and Daniel Craig ever since I heard them purr, "Bond. James Bond." I'm a sucker for men with British accents and men who look good in tuxedos, men who don't require me to make them dinner or do their laundry.

What's not to like? Bonds are like wild, exotic animals. Elusive, dangerous, powerful, elegant . . . sexy. A kiss from one of them and you're sure to be swept off your feet faster than you can whisper, "Shaken, not stirred." Oh, yes—007 has skills.

My only issue with Bond is that none of them ever chose a mom to be their lovely, provocatively named Bond Girl. I'll have you know, after endless revisions, I finally settled on a provocative name that fits me perfectly—"Dusty Drawers."

Why pick me, you ask? Well, I'm smart, savvy, well-seasoned. And I have something those ultra-slim sirens who came before me don't have—Spanx. That's right, just think of the weaponry, coloring books and nonperishable items I could hide in there.

And, I've got skills, too—Super Momma Skills—such as eyes in the back of my head and super-sonic hearing. When voices drop to a whisper, my radar goes up faster than you can turn on a dust buster. I'm also impervious to pain, for I have walked on Legos. Barefoot.

Those heightened senses can be found in any mom, especially one raising teenagers. I am acutely aware when someone wants something (especially money) or is hiding something (like the truth) or just ate candy (remember, heightened senses). More importantly, I'm dangerous and mysterious; just ask the ladies at See's Candies. They never know what I'm going to ask for when I come in. I like to keep them on their toes. Uh-huh. Dan-ger-ous.

Like most moms, I can do all those things a young beautiful Bond girl can do, and then some. Not only can I look quite fetching in an A-line ballgown *with* sleeves, I can run in heels—preferably low ones—and catch things flung at my head in midair while driving. (Anyone who's had a toddler knows what I mean.) And I can do it all without sleep, which, if you're doing the math, I haven't had since 1990. I am a mom, after all. That's how we roll.

You're probably wondering if this delicate, albeit delusional, mom-creature can handle a weapon. Well, you and MI6 can rest assured that from what I have been told, I am quite handy with gadgets. I'm not bad with a Panini maker, either.

Oh, yes, Mr. Bond, with a mom on your team, you would be in good hands. And I can guarantee the job would get done faster than you could say, "What's up, pretty lady?" Not that Bond would ever say that.

I might not be as young and as lovely as the women 007 is used to frolicking with, but I think Bond is ready for a mature woman like me. We have a lot in common, you know. We're both in our 40s, we both use eye cream, and after a stressful day making the world a better, safer place, we both could use a good stiff martini.

And when you think you're done, a new day begins. The good thing is one day you will catch your breath and catch up on your sleep; it's called being an empty nester. Then you will have plenty of time to work it like a Bond Girl should.

Alarm buzzes . . . back to reality.

Later, James.

Linda dreaming about being a
Bond Girl

You Did What?!

Let nothing surprise you!

Dear Colleen —
Moms unite!
Enjoy~
Jenny

Holey Moley

by
Jenny Beatrice

Today's mothers of teenagers have to be prepared to respond to some outlandish requests, such as, "Can you buy me another cellphone because I dropped mine in the toilet again?" and, "Can I try out for *American Idol*?" and, "Can I have $300,000 for college?" My personal favorite is, "Can I use my face as a dartboard?"

I spent most of my teen years unsuccessfully attempting to keep weird bumps and holes from appearing on my face, but by the looks of today's pierced and poked teenagers, it seems my bad complexion was a style ahead of its time.

My daughter Madeleine was 15 when she asked to have her nose pierced. Of course I said no, as any good mother would do. Besides, she had zero tolerance for pain and a subzero desire to follow directions. She earned this reputation when she had her ears pierced a few years earlier. That event resulted in the disgusting extraction of an earring that had become embedded deep in her lobe . . . performed by yours truly—Nurse Ratched. We were both scarred for life.

So while "Good Mom" was shouting "NO!" on one shoulder, "Bad Mom"—the one with six holes of her own—was shouting "YES!" I admit I have my share of excess holes in my body. My love for ear bling began in eighth grade when I wanted a second ear piercing on one side. With my powers of persuasion, I convinced my mother it made good fiscal sense because I could wear all those lonely earrings that had lost their mates. From there it went to two in both ears then three in one ear. The reason? I had been diagnosed with a touch of scoliosis, so I explained the extra weight on one side was a medical necessity.

I have no excuse—medical or otherwise—for hole number six, a cartilage piercing that I got in my late 20s when I was already the mother of two. Did I not have enough oozing holes on my hands with two babies? Eventually, coordinating all those earrings every day was like trying to herd very tiny cats, and I gave up. Once or twice a year, when I feel like being the hippest mom in the high-school parking lot, I force an earring in my upper ear. This fashion statement lasts about an hour because my ear itches with a vengeance and the post pokes my skull when I'm on business calls.

This is why young adults should think more about their future employment and less about putting holes in their faces, body parts and internal organs. Most adults say that you can't get a job with gauges dragging your earlobes down to your kneecaps or with eyebrow metal picking up AM radio. I am here to say that today's youth will not be so lucky. Kids, you will be forced to have a job, and that ass piercing of yours is going to smart when you are stuck at your desk in your non-ergonomic chair for nine hours. And one day, you will sneeze at a breakfast meeting and your nose ring will be propelled across the room and directly onto your boss's cream-cheese bagel. Work is painful enough without all that hardware getting in the way.

I tried to talk Madeleine out of the nose piercing using my proven powers of persuasion, but my words of wisdom went in one hole and out the other. She responded with a whiny litany of reasons why the nose ring was going to make her miserable life worth living and an even longer litany of promises she would fulfill in return for my permission. Despite her begging and pleading, yelling and screaming, I stood my ground. "Bad Mom" was being squeezed out by "Perimenopausal Mom," a tired old woman who was physically incapable of agreeing to anything—ever.

Like any good daughter, she ignored me and turned to her father. With her Daddy's-Little-Girl eyes, she mesmerized him with notions of being the "cool parent." He caved in record time, but tried to regain some parental control by insisting he would be the one to take her to get it done. So they went off to the finest piercing shop on the local "hip strip," and I stayed home wondering if this was some twisted bonding experience that has come to replace the father-daughter dance.

Madeline is now a respectable college student with a job and a nose ring. Her nose has not gangrened. She has not run off and joined the circus. No adults have shaken their index fingers in her face to say, "If only you didn't have that nose ring, you'd be a beautiful girl." And she is beautiful. I have to admit it looks great. In fact, it suits her so well that you hardly notice it is there—that is until allergy season when a nose ring lands on your cream-cheese bagel.

Mom with Madeleine showing off her nose ring

A Monitored Heart

by
Emily Rich

About two years after I finished chemotherapy I had to be fitted with a portable heart monitor. It was a temporary arrangement to determine if Tamoxifen—the drug I was taking post breast cancer—was giving me heart palpitations. The oncologist, who I was still seeing every three months for follow-ups, raised her eyebrows slightly when, in response to her question, I told her that maybe my heartbeat felt irregular sometimes, but it was no big deal.

I think oncologists must all be a little inscrutable, walking around all day with files of information—maybe heartening, maybe devastating—for some poor cancer patient. So when I tried to take back my comment about heart palpitations, make it into a joke about being a mother of teenagers ("Ha ha! Who wouldn't have heart troubles, right?"), her reaction was stoic and hard to read.

But she told me I needed to go immediately to see a cardiologist. She would put in a call. It was a Friday afternoon, already nearing time for the kids to get home from school.

"Can I wait until Monday?" I asked.

She shook her head. "Tamoxifen can sometimes cause dangerous blood clots," she explained. I needed to have my heart looked at right away.

Already my pulse was racing. I texted Rachael, my 16-year-old. "Can you get Harper from school? I'm still at the doctor's office."

"Yeah, no prob," she replied. "Can I go out after?"

My beautiful, talented and maddeningly adventurous middle child had spent more of her high-school years being grounded than otherwise. And though tonight she was free, it was always with a twinge of anxiety that I let that girl out of my sight.

"Be home by midnight," I replied, thumbs tapping against the BlackBerry keyboard.

"Thanks, Mom! Oh, and r u OK?"

"I'm fine. Just some more tests to do. Don't worry."

It was after six by the time I got home, too late to start dinner. When my husband, Curt, got home from work a little while later, we ordered Thai food and opened a bottle of wine.

"Look at this stupid thing they're making me wear," I said, lifting up my shirt to reveal the electrodes—six of them—affixed to my chest and ribcage, connected with black wires to a hard plastic recording device on a belt around my waist.

"And look," I continued, holding up the wallet-sized paper booklet I'd been given, "I have to keep a journal and write down any activity that 'elevates my heart rate.'"

"Well, we might try to get your heart racing a little later

tonight," Curt said, grinning. He gave my thigh a squeeze. But we fell asleep on the couch, as usual, and shuffled off to the bedroom only after our son Harper emerged from the basement sometime around 11 o'clock.

At midnight, Rachael came in to tell us she was home, and I listened as she climbed the stairs to her room. Which is when the insomnia set in.

In the first place, the whole heart-monitor contraption made it uncomfortable to sleep. In addition, the Tamoxifen-fueled hot flashes burned with particular intensity.

In bed, I watched the blades of the ceiling fan turn languidly overhead. Next to me, Curt was in a deep sleep, lying like a pharaoh on his back, his breath steady, measured. When I was sick and in chemo, his sleep was restless, and he would startle awake like a child then pat his hand across my belly or hip to make sure I was still there. He slept more soundly now that the worst was over.

I didn't want to wake him with my restlessness, so I slid off the bed and headed to the bathroom. Standing before the mirror, lit only by the dim glow of the streetlight, I took a brief inventory. I was 45 years old, two years out of treatment. My hair was back. Thick, loose curls now reached my shoulders. One breast was gone, replaced by an implant that sat high and pert under my pajama camisole. My skin was covered with the sheen of sweat. The first two electrodes from the heart monitor were clearly visible just below both collarbones.

In a way, I blamed myself for my medical predicament. My mother was first diagnosed with breast cancer at age 56. I'd known her condition put me at risk, that genetically I was predisposed to get the disease, and yet I'd been cavalier about getting screened.

"Aren't you supposed to get a mammogram every year?" Curt would ask. "You know, because of your mom?"

"Yeah, but I'm not like my mom," would be my reply, thinking of her poor health choices and her decision to remain with my abusive father to the end of her life.

When the kids were little and my health was fine, I had a delusional belief in my ability to control my own destiny. *If I make good lifestyle choices with healthy habits and strong relationships,* I thought, *I will steer myself and my happy little family safely through the scary shoals of life.*

There is nothing like teenagers and disease to quickly dispel a person of such a delusion.

In fact . . . *what's that noise coming from upstairs?*

I paused then moved closer to the air duct leading from my bathroom to Rachael's room. There it was again, distinctly heard, a male voice coming from upstairs—too deep to be Harper's.

Quietly, I moved into the hallway and up the narrow set of stairs that led to the kids' rooms. As I moved up the wooden steps, the heart monitor clinging to me like a baby gibbon, I kept my ears honed in on any suspicious sounds coming from Rachael's room at the end of the hall.

The soft click of a door being locked sent a surge of parental rage through me. I quickened my pace, flicked on the hall light and pounded on her door.

"Rachael! Open this door this instant!" I could practically feel the valves of my heart swelling with angry, rushing blood.

The door opened a crack, and a sliver of Rachael's face appeared.

"Hey, Mom, I was just going to the bathroom, and . . ."

"Open your door. Now."

After a sigh and a sheepish look, the door swung open to reveal Rachael standing in a tiny T-shirt and the boy-cut pajama shorts I'd bought her in New York. Her long dark hair was tousled, her skin glowing and awake.

Beyond her, between the dresser and the shelf of basketball trophies, I could see the crouching figure of her young male friend. He was dressed, thank God, in jeans and a white T-shirt, his hair pushed back into the stylish swoop he always wore. The sight of him cowering only further enraged me, but I managed, in a firm but controlled voice, to tell him, "Get out of my house. Now."

He whooshed by me, with his head down, and bolted for the stairs.

Rachael and I remained in her doorway, her expression now hardened into defiance.

"Rachael! What the hell?!" I snapped. Air moved furiously through my nostrils, and my lips were pushed into a frown as I steeled myself for the Mom-and-Rachael screaming match I was certain was about to erupt.

Instead, I watched her expression soften and her dark eyes widen as they landed on the electrodes poking out of my pajama top.

"Oh, my God, Mom! What happened?"

I looked down at my chest then back at my daughter. "It's a heart monitor. The doctors want to make sure I don't have a blood clot."

"Mom!" Now it was her turn to be accusatory. "Why

didn't you tell me? I thought you said you were OK!"

Somehow her indignation warmed and pacified me—as if my rebellious body and daughter had both been stilled right there on the blue-carpeted threshold of Rachael's room.

"I think I'm OK," I told her. "I mean, honestly, I don't feel like there's anything wrong." And then I added, "But I'm going to have to write about this episode in my heart-rate journal."

She had no idea what I was talking about, but laughed anyway. "Do whatcha gotta do, Mom."

It turned out I did not have a blood clot after all. In fact, over the 72 hours of monitoring, the cardiologist could detect nothing irregular with my heart. By the time I went in for the follow-up exam, the whole nighttime incident with Rachael had moved from infuriating to exasperatingly funny in my mind, and I pointed out the entry in my heart-rate journal without embarrassment.

"I had to chase a boy out of my daughter's room at one in the morning," I told the cardiologist.

The older, gray-haired, distinguished man looked down at the journal, bemused. "Well, it didn't raise your pulse to a degree that would signal any kind of problem." He looked up from the booklet. "I've raised three kids myself and have been through three teenagers. You gotta be strong in here." He tapped his chest in a way that indicated he was talking about more than just cardio function. "Gotta have a strong heart to get through it."

NYMB . . . On Being a Mom

So Little Wine

by
Sioux Roslawski

"Mom, what side is the Arch on? Is it on the Missouri side or the Illinois side?"

This was one of the many moments that made me so proud to be Ian's mother. It was also one of the instances that made me—every four to six weeks—go to the store and buy a box of hair dye, hoping this time it would miraculously cover all the gray. But with a kid like Ian, nothing made by Clairol or L'Oreal was powerful enough.

My beloved 18-year-old son, a straight-A student, was repeatedly driving back and forth across the Mississippi River. His ultimate destination was a concert on the east side, so he was well aware he was headed to Illinois. However, he kept turning around and driving back and forth across the bridge. Now the Arch was on his right side . . . now it was on his left. He was getting confused, and I was getting frustrated. How could he be so clueless about his location?

To be fair, St. Louis is located right on the border between the two states, and our home is a mere five minutes from the Illinois state line. There are times we head to a department store in Illinois because it's closer than one in our home state. And yes, the Arch almost—but not quite—spans both states, but its legs are quite rooted in Missouri soil.

Then there's the name that should have been Ian's clue: The St. Louis Gateway Arch. This kid of mine had taken honors classes in high school and had won a substantial music scholarship to a private college, and yet he was completely bamboozled by the geography of his hometown.

After I had served as Ian's personal GPS, he found his way to the concert, had a wonderful time and returned safe and sound and on gas fumes. I guess all those laps back and forth across the muddy Mississippi really sucked up the gasoline.

Since my whining had never made much of an impact on this fruit of my loins, the next afternoon I didn't whine—I had a glass of wine instead. It wasn't the first time Ian had made me want to yank my hair out . . . and I felt quite sure it wouldn't be the last.

As I drained the dregs from my wineglass, I remembered when Ian was a junior in high school and I was teaching in a neighboring district. On the second-to-last day of school one year, my son was bubbling over. Two days away from beginning his fun-filled summer vacation, all Ian could focus on was how he was going to sleep in, how he was going to play tennis and football all day and how he was going to play computer games all night.

Most kids would have expressed their excitement through

laughter and talking too loudly to their friends. They might have danced down the halls in school as they traveled from class to class. But my son was different from most kids.

Coming in the front door that afternoon after school, his book bag hanging from one shoulder, my brilliant boy told me, "I got suspended from school." Immediately, my blood pressure soared to near-stroke level. Images of Ian getting in a fight flew through my head, even though he had never been in an altercation with a classmate. Instead of relying on his fists, he used his sense of humor to diffuse tense situations.

OK, calm down, I told myself, *it probably wasn't a fight.* Visions of my son becoming belligerent and speaking disrespectfully to a teacher filled my brain. Maybe his mouth got him into this mess. He could be quite sarcastic (from his father's genetic contribution, you understand) and often had to curb his tongue. Fond of arguing, my child's habit of constantly questioning things made everything from mealtimes to family reunions to vacations an unbroken string of debates.

"Suspended? What do you mean you're suspended? What in the hell happened?!"

From his perspective, I probably looked like I could have stunt-doubled for Godzilla. Several rows of teeth emerged. Fiery breath exploded from my mouth. My eyes blazed a crazy shade of crimson and my front paws were up and ready—and those claws of mine were razor-sharp.

Apparently, the incident happened in the cafeteria. My 6-foot-tall son was so wound up about the end of the school year that he morphed into a human bowling ball. After sliding across the tiled floor, he crashed into several garbage cans, causing food scraps and half-filled milk cartons and slop to spill onto the floor.

"What about your finals, Ian? You've got tests to take tomorrow." My voice shook. I considered my options: If I committed a felony right then and twisted his head off his neck, wouldn't that mean I'd have unlimited time to read while I was in prison?

"Oh, they had me take them this afternoon before I left," he said. "I'm all done."

And so was my anger. My red-hot rage quickly dissipated. Certainly, I didn't want him to think I condoned what he had done. Being suspended was—from my viewpoint—never something to laugh about. But getting kicked out of school because he bowled his way across the commons and made a mess . . . well, it seemed a bit silly.

Before school administrators, teachers and rigid parents of supposedly blameless children start frothing at the mouth about policies and procedures and exceptions that cannot be made, please listen. I get it. I do. I'm a teacher myself, but I wonder if making him clean up his mess—along with the mess that all the lunch shifts made—might have been a more appropriate consequence.

So I didn't chuckle at the silliness. Instead, I told him, "Well, you were so thrilled about school almost being over, and now it is. How fortunate for you." I walked away so he wouldn't see my half-smile.

And then of course there were memories of his antics with the marching band. I poured myself *another* glass of wine.

Having taken private music lessons since he was in seventh

grade, Ian's musical skills were impressive—his performances made me puff up with pride as a pleased mama. Seeing him march across the football field with his flashy brass trumpet and listening as he soloed in competitions delighted me.

But as he was dressing for the marching band shows, I was less than delighted. Every time he prepared to perform at a football game or a competitive show, we'd get into a shout-fest. The problem? His hair.

Regional regulations meant that all the participants' hair—both male and female—had to be either very short or tucked under their hats. Because my son's hair dusted his shoulders, something had to be done with it.

The easiest solution would have been to get a haircut, but my son hardly ever did anything the simple way. The next simplest idea: wear a hairnet. My child wouldn't even consider that one—too lunch-lady for his tastes. Barrettes, headbands, stocking caps . . . we tried them all.

Much to my dismay, the girls in the band found a way to fix the problem. When Ian walked out of the school building one day to get onto the bus for the marching-band show, his hair was indeed up and off his collar—in a couple of dozen tiny pigtails. Pink, blue, green, purple and yellow rubber bands held the little tufts of hair in place. He looked ridiculous, but since he had gotten lots of attention from the young women, and since his hair problem was now solved, he didn't care.

Of course, his driving escapades didn't begin with his marathon trip back and forth across the Mississippi. One time, my baby boy got a ticket for rolling through a stop sign. He swore he looked to his left, looked to his right and looked straight ahead to ensure it was safe to roll on through without braking completely. The only direction he didn't check was behind him—and directly behind him was a police officer.

So many memories, so little wine. Time to open another bottle . . .

A Change of Tune

by
Debra Ayers Brown

I'd always been protective of my only child. But, as Mom reminded me, Meredith would be heading to college next year so maybe I should consider taking her and her friend Lizzie to the Projekt Revolution tour, headlined by some of her favorite bands. *Seriously, what could happen?* I thought.

I should've had an inkling when we left Savannah's triple-digit August heat wave and headed to "Hotlanta." The four-hour drive passed without incident until we hit Atlanta traffic and I missed the hotel exit. I made a frantic call to the hotel concierge for directions—all while driving 90 miles an hour with the traffic.

What was I thinking? I hate driving in Atlanta. And now I had two teens squealing in the back seat, thrilled to be going to an outdoor amphitheater for a hard-rock concert.

My thoughts wandered to my first concert in the mid-1970s,

still memorable like a first kiss, a rite of passage. I'd rushed in with friends when the doors opened, pushing to the front by the stage. Speaker stacks throbbed. Acrid cigarette smoke rose to the lights. Beer tabs popped. It was all so worldly to this small-town girl with hands held high, jumping to the beat.

I treasured the memory even now, but I'd missed any backstage drug use or drunken brawls I'd read about later. *Will Meredith be lucky enough to miss them, too?*

As we whipped through downtown traffic, my worrywart side took over. Amid calling the hotel concierge repeatedly, I made a mental list of what could happen at this multigroup concert:

A) Meredith could become a groupie, run away with a tattooed rocker and I'd have to tell her dad.

B) Lizzie could become a groupie, run away with a tattooed rocker and I'd have to face her mom.

C) Meredith and Lizzie could become groupies, run away with tattooed rockers and I'd have to join them, shouting, "Party on!"

My mind reeled with endless possibilities—all bad.

"Quit worrying," Meredith said from the backseat. "We'll get to the hotel soon, and you can relax."

And I did rest after check-in—until I met with the hotel concierge to discuss the next morning's logistical concerns and transportation options.

"They're expecting a mob scene," he informed me, cocking a brow, obviously thinking I had lost my mind. He seemed to remember my frantic calls for directions. All 12,000 of them. But I refused to be intimidated by the snooty guy in the pinstripe suit with a touch of gray at his temples. I had bigger worries.

"You should stay in your room," he ordered. "We'll arrange for a responsible driver to take them to and from the event."

The driver arrived on time the next morning. Meredith and Lizzie, dressed to the rocker nines, climbed in a black town car and disappeared.

I had plenty of time to rethink my decision to let them go alone. Off and on, mercury-topping temperature alerts popped up on the TV screen. Reporters broke into broadcasts to discuss heat-related deaths. Before regular programming returned, they cut away to the concert, showing lots of tattooed guys partying with rocker chicks.

I decided to keep my cool by raiding the hotel minifridge, soaking in the tub and trying to forget about the girls. A little me-time felt pretty darn good as scented bubble bath filled the air and a $10 peanut M&M melted in my mouth. Warm water sloshed against my body, lulling me into a sense of well-being. I zoned out, thinking, *Seriously, what could happen?*

My cellphone jarred me out of my bliss. I danced out of the tub, slid across the wet floor and banged my arm against the countertop in a dash to the bedroom.

"Baby?" I noticed Meredith's number displayed on the cell.

"Hi, Mom," a raspy male voice said, punctuated by clangs, loud chatter and rowdy laughter.

"Who is this?" I asked. "Where's Meredith?"

"I have no idea," he said. "I'm with MCR." He paused, and

I gulped. "Someone tossed her phone from the mosh pit to Jimmy Urine, lead singer of Mindless Self Indulgence, and he called the dad on her contact list from the stage. But no one answered."

"Jimmy Urine?" I repeated. Really? You couldn't make this stuff up. Where was my easy-listening station when I needed it?

He chuckled. "So I thought I'd call Mom," he said, "and try to get a return address."

I gave him the requested info and preened about talking to a guy from MCR until I realized Meredith had no phone. Then I felt nothing. Nada. Nil. Zilch. Except mind-blowing panic.

What could happen indeed!

Two hours later, two exhausted but exhilarated teens wearing MCR T-shirts rolled in. Tales of first-time crowd surfing led to the lost cellphone confession.

"It fell off my belt clip," Meredith admitted. "Well-intentioned but ultimately wrong young men kept carrying us out of the pit." She took a deep breath before continuing her rant. "We're young, feminist women! We wanted to mosh." She ran her hands through her sweat-soaked hair. "We needed to stay in the pit."

I stared at them, dumbfounded, thankful they'd made it home. Thankful, too, that the rocker dude hadn't reached her dad.

"It was so cool," Lizzie said and slung her long blond hair back and forth.

Meredith followed with head banging then said, "We borrowed a phone to call our driver."

"He fell asleep," Lizzie chimed in. "But Meredith didn't

panic. She kept calling him. She's persistent . . . like you."

She turned to Meredith, who was either on the verge of getting a serious grounding or a pat on the back for conquering the obstacles set before her.

Grounding seemed imminent, but I kept silent.

The next morning, I changed my tune. I realized she was her mother's daughter and could handle whatever came her way.

"College should be a breeze now," I said, thinking of Meredith's upcoming solo act.

Though the cellphone never arrived in the mail, the concert experience smoothed the way for Meredith's transition from home to college for both of us. She had the confidence to embrace college life and live in the dorm. And I knew she'd always find her way home.

Independence rocked.

Marked for Life

by
Linda O'Connell

When my children were small, I adamantly disapproved of rub-on tattoos. When they came home from birthday parties, I rifled through their goody bags. Sure, I snatched a piece of candy or two, but my quest was for those fake tattoos that some dumb mom thought were cute and harmless party favors.

If the kids rubbed them on their bodies, I scrubbed them off. I considered transfer tattoos precursors to permanent branding, and I vowed not be a party to the defacing of my kids' bodies. They did enough of that on their own—my son was a billboard of scrapes, scabs and scars, and my daughter sported too-orange blush, clashing pink lipstick and hideous fashions.

Kids are fickle at age 15; if they had imprinted the names of their latest sweethearts on their bodies, there would have been weekly scratch-outs and replacement names up and down their arms. I couldn't prevent their weekly heartbreak, but I was able to prevent their future pain of tattoo removal. As they got older, I simply said, "NO!" to permanent tattoos.

Times have changed. Nowadays, I cringe when I see my grandchildren sporting a temporary Spidey on their forearms. What can I say when they shove some superhero under my nose and ask me what I think? If I told them, I'd never get Grandma visitation, so I direct their attention to my own "tattoo."

Don't get me wrong. I wasn't a willing participant. In fact, I was so mad at my new husband when I discovered the half-dollar-sized indigo-blue heart shape on my lower left leg that I screamed. "Bill, what have you done to me?!"

"Married you on Valentine's Day and made you my wife," the big joker laughed. His playful nature and sense of humor had drawn me to him. I liked my funny honey, but I did not appreciate being drawn on.

"You know how I feel about tattoos." I grimaced. He watched me spit and rub. He observed as I scoured and scrubbed. But the image remained.

"What did you do—use permanent ink when you drew this?"

"Honey, I didn't do it. Let me see your leg."

I raised my leg and shoved my foot into his gut. "Look what you did! I can't get it off."

"Now calm down. I didn't draw on you. Take a closer look and tell me what you really think."

"I think I love you, but I'm 40 years old, and I don't want a teeny-bopper tattoo to prove it."

I looked closely at my shin and gasped as the realization sunk in that no amount of cleanser or intense scrubbing—nothing—could remove it, short of a visit to the dermatologist. One of my spider veins had broken into a clearly defined, perfect heart shape. I was marked for life.

Nowadays, when my grandchildren show me their tattoos, I hike my pant leg and take each child aside individually and say, "See Nana's tattoo? I got this one to show the world how much I love YOU. But shhh! Don't tell the other kids."

Scene of the Slime

by
Terri Spilman

"Mommy, you killed Roxie!"

Insert. Knife. Twist. In. Heart.

I never thought the little girl who wrote love notes to me every day would ever accuse me of being a cold-blooded snail murderess. Yes, Roxie is a snail.

How was I to know? Who died and made me Jacques Cousteau? Nowhere in my 1000-page *How to Care For Your Child from Newborn to 5 Years* handbook—yes, Grace did come complete with a how-to book from the hospital—was there a chapter called, "How to Care for a Pet Snail."

Ironically, I always thought the snail was a murderess. Six goldfish also in the aquarium with Roxie mysteriously died one-by-one after the Easter Bunny brought them to our house last year. Roxie never seemed shaken whenever there was a floater. Was it a coincidence that they were last seen near the pink castle this snail called home?

Something was definitely fishy. Roxie was a sly one, and a bit of a recluse. The only time we saw her was when she half emerged from her shell to eat, and, of course, to kill goldfish.

I often feared Roxie would die of starvation. The mom in me was worried about how to feed a snail—I had no idea. And, I have to admit, I was totally jealous of the fact that Roxie could eat whatever she wanted and never have to bust out of her shell. I, on the other hand, have to constantly monitor everything I eat as I've busted out of more than my share of mom jeans over the years from seemingly slight overindulgences.

My eight-year-old Grace adored Roxie, the queen of the underwater pink castle. That is, she was queen until she was murdered—I mean, until she died peacefully.

It was Grace's responsibility to care for her aquarium, but school and after-school activities took precedence in her life. The aquarium's water became so dirty that Roxie's bright pink castle was barely visible in the murk. But I wasn't going to clean it—it was important to teach my daughter a lesson about caring for a pet. Unfortunately, the tank became too dirty and Roxie went to sleep. For good.

Just as TV's Cosby family gave its goldfish a respectful, loving send-off complete with a prayer service and royal flush down the toilet, we needed to do something for Roxie. However, what do you do with a dead snail besides make broth? Who am I, the Travel Channel's bizarre food guru Andrew Zimmern? Of course not. I'm just a mother expected to be part zoologist and part funeral director.

I couldn't really flush Roxie down our low-flow toilet. She'd never get to the nearby river and would cost us a fortune due to a visit from Mr. Rooter. So, we decided to put Roxie in the garden. That is, until Dogzilla, our very hungry Golden Retriever, channeled her inner French poodle and tried to dine on a little escargot.

One child meltdown later, Roxie was saved and placed in a Brighton heart-shaped tin. It was the perfect tomb for Roxie to be laid to rest. We placed her shell-side up in the tin and as we put the lid on, Grace wanted to take one last look. Reluctantly, I turned Roxie over and, by God, I thought I saw a tentacle move.

My daughter saw the same thing. It was like those stories when an arm pops up out of a casket at a funeral home viewing.

Holy crap! Was the snail still alive? How can you tell if a snail is dead?

I couldn't, in good conscience, keep Roxie in the tin if there was a chance she was still alive. So we put her in some water and both stared. Nothing. It turned out to be a false alarm.

After placing the tin into the ground and covering it with dirt, Grace placed a sign on Roxie's grave. We then said a prayer along with our last goodbyes.

So now Roxie rests safely in her heart-shaped box, enduring sleet, rain and snow.

I tried to comfort Grace as much as I could over her loss. Thankfully, a neighborhood girl gave my daughter a stuffed snail—Beanie Baby-stuffed, not garlic- and bread crumbs-stuffed. All has been forgiven.

I'm back on the love note list again and cleared from the scene of the slime—that is, until karma rears its ugly head and I never hear the end of it when she becomes a teenager.

For now, I'll cherish my mommy love notes.

Above: Roxie's pink castle and (R) Roxie's final resting place

A Mother's Expectations

by
Marcia Gaye

Mothers have expectations. As soon as a woman finds out she's expecting, hopes gestate right along with the baby. The very word "expecting" makes it kind of obvious. We start birthing these hopes way before the gurney rolls us into the delivery room, these premature, underweight glimmers of motherhood as we imagine it will be.

Our babies will giggle and coo and talk in complete sentences before they grow teeth that won't need braces. We'll have children who love carrot sticks in their lunchboxes and who never wipe their noses on their sleeves or the guest towel. Because we will be such awesome parents, our teenagers will love to learn, be trustworthy and responsible and share all about their day around the dinner table each evening.

Horror stories recited by older, wiser parents, like nursery rhymes that warn of pain and suffering, glance off our super-mom armor with nary a scuff mark.

Then at 16, my son came home with a handful of green Kool-Aid packets and announced he was going to dye his hair. That's one scenario I hadn't envisioned.

I am a cool mom. I'd been a flower child myself, not quite anarchist enough to be a hippie, but a freethinker in fringe. I was interested. *Why green?* I wondered. And, *What will I do with him after he is expelled?*

When I was young, there was a movie, *The Boy with Green Hair.* The details escape me, except for a boy crying while his hair was being shaved because all the kids taunted him. And once he was bald, you knew those same mean kids were going to taunt him for that, too.

My son had not seen the movie.

I knew before I even asked that there was no answer to, "Why do you want to dye your hair green?" He heard through the high-school grapevine that Kool-Aid was the stuff to use. So I confiscated it.

But then, cool mom that I am, I ran the kitchen sink full of hot water, sprinkled all the packets in and helped him lie on his back on the kitchen counter so he could dip his head backward into the lime slime.

That's where it got tricky.

My son has brown hair, thick and wiry. His hair didn't take well to the dye. He lay there longer. He complained his neck was getting stiff. I dabbed his forehead and cheeks with a cold, damp cloth. He thought I was being thoughtful, but I was actually in a panic because his skin was turning green. At least I thought it looked green under the red flush caused by his being tilted backward for half an hour.

I finally furnished an old towel and assisted my sweet, smart, talented child to a chair where we waited for his blood flow to stabilize.

Around his face, where his hair used to be a lovely shade of gold, it now had the patina of tarnished verdi copper. And his sideburns were definitely green. The rest of his hair was just as brown as before. I sighed with vague relief. *Perhaps he won't be expelled.*

The next week, in bopped his sister, elegant in a new asymmetrical haircut. One side brushed her shoulder, the other her chin. Her hair was a beautiful shade of purple. Eggplant, she clarified.

Deciding she wanted something even more dramatic, she asked me to shave the underneath section, nape to earlobe . . . into a purple modified *Three Stooges'* Moe Howard bowl cut on one side.

Sure, I am a cool mom. Of course I encouraged individual expression in my children. I gulped.

So while the clippers hummed, I reconsidered those early expectations of motherhood, those fantasy hopes that make pregnancy bearable. In all those preconceived scenarios, I never once pictured myself shaving my daughter's head or brushing my son's long green hair.

Being a mom is all about surprises that surpass imagination, that catapult us to levels of joy and pain for which we are completely unprepared. We birth our child once, yet every day thereafter brings new experiences. What fun not to know in advance what those experiences will be!

Marcia's son Nathaniel Jobe, on his high school graduation day, free flowing hair noted

Case of the Condom Culprit

by
Lesley Morgan

We are a blended family. My husband has two sons from his previous marriage, and I have two from mine.

Being a mom to four boys is challenging under normal circumstances, but being a stepmom can require the practice of diplomacy at the level of détente. Our sons are adults now, but their adolescent years created some interesting family dynamics, especially in the blame department. Even now, when food gets dropped on the Oriental carpet or a favorite sweatshirt goes missing, someone jokingly accuses, "Jon did it," even though Jon is miles away.

During our shared parenting years, despite valiant attempts to present a unified front, my husband and I would occasionally find ourselves on opposite sides of the who-did-it debate. We couldn't admit our own darlings were guilty, so we'd run through all possible persons of interest in a way that would make Robert Stack proud. Here is one of our great unsolved mysteries:

About seven years ago, we were moving to another part of the state. We put our mulching worms up for adoption and set aside things that were destined for the dump—moldy sports equipment, expired food, hopelessly stained clothing, broken electronics, patched tires and a cat condo built with recycled carpet from our neighbor's trash.

My husband and I were moving a dog-chewed loveseat out of the teen cave that was our basement when we discovered two sticky (ewww!) stiff condoms under one of the cushions. We expected to find loose change, cat toys or even old food like M&M's or pretzels, but not the residue of a long-forgotten tryst—not in *our* house where stealth surveillance of post-midnight arrivals and Internet traffic was raised to an art form.

We were both dismayed and disgusted by our discovery, and the finger pointing began immediately. Couched in denial, my husband and I began the process of elimination.

At that time, our four boys were between the ages of 19 and 25—any one of them could have been guilty. But we knew, without a doubt, that it didn't involve two of them:

1) My older son was an ultraorthodox Jew, who practiced a "no touch" policy. In his religion, Chassidic law prohibits physical contact with members of the opposite sex prior to marriage, though kissing your mom is OK. Plus, he hadn't stayed at our house with a young lady for at least three years

prior to his conversion. If the condoms had been his, they would have petrified with age. Still, even the most righteous among us had been tested . . . and failed. I guess I lost my Good Housekeeping Seal of Approval when I forgot to vacuum under the cushions.

2) My husband's older son was living in Washington, D.C. at the time and working for a law firm. Though he had brought his girlfriend to the house as recently as Christmas, he was too smart to leave evidence lying around.

Hopefully, all of our boys were smart enough to take out their trash. Obviously, we had some rethinking to do, so we considered the last two boys on our family roster:

3) At the time of our discovery, my younger son was using the room in question as a bedroom and as a gathering spot for his friends. He moved in when our oldest boy moved out, adding a big TV, black lights, strobes and strings of chaser lights, the type that brings on seizures. And he had painted "Club 305" with glow-in-the-dark paint on the outside of the door, as a sort of bring-it-on party alert.

Consequently, hoards of young men and women had pressed their hot bodies together in various platonic combinations on the couches and floor during marathons with the DVD game series *Scene It*. How else could 19 people fit in an area with an occupancy limit of six? In fact, on many occasions, couples had been left alone at the house while our son and others went on pizza runs. This led us to consider my younger son's girlfriend who was a regular member of Club 305.

My husband's finger started wagging big time, so we decided to question the one son who was currently living in our house. With his girlfriend beside him, we broke the news of the condom.

"Hey, son. We were removing the couch and found two used condoms under the cushions. Are they yours?" I asked. No beating around the bush here.

My younger son's face went sincerely blank, as if coping with incomprehension. Then he winced, and his mouth twisted with revulsion. Shaking his head, he replied, "No, Mom. Ugh! If I'd known, I wouldn't have sat there. Besides, we always sit on the other couch."

This was true. We hadn't found condoms there.

Concurrent with this exchange, his girlfriend's mouth was frozen in a big "O" of disbelief and distaste. Her shoulders were scrunched, as if she expected to be hit with more bad news, like the discovery of used Maxi pads or wads of snot.

Their spontaneous reactions seemed entirely innocent to me. My husband, however, was shaking his head and clearly overestimated their acting abilities. My eyes narrowed as my motherly instincts kicked into high gear to protect my child, to the point that I considered starching my hubby's underwear.

With an air of "It isn't over until it's over," we left the room and moved on.

4) We considered my husband's younger son, who was a bit of a player. He had spent a lot of time with females on

the loveseat in question—without a chaperone, of course. He flirted with any cute thing in a skirt, so I refused to cross him off my list of suspects. I enunciated "flirted" with heavy implications, but my irony was lost on my spouse who simply dotes on this boy.

The topic came up for discussion yet again the following morning when my husband reached into the pocket of the suit he was wearing to work. Wide-eyed, he pulled out an over-sized Lifesaver snuggled within a condom-sized wrapper. The forgotten mint made him frown.

"You know, you really should reconsider the evidence," he said, "especially where your younger son is concerned. Would you like me to draw a Venn diagram to show all of the possibilities?"

"You're kidding," I countered incredulously. And with my arms crossed and defiant, I insisted that his son could as easily be blamed.

Some more debate followed—brief, but tense. Finally, we compromised and named the guilty parties Ramses and Ramona, a phantom couple that was left alone during a pizza-foraging mission. And thus, we put the matter to bed.

In conclusion, I've one thing to add: the next time we find a surprise under a seat cushion, I'm hoping it's a winning Powerball ticket.

Lessons in Motherhood

You're never too old to learn.

Mom Got Back

by
Dawn Weber

I have been strongly encouraged not to sing. Ever. And I'm not sure why. I'm a great singer.

Who do I sound like, you ask? Carrie Underwood? Katy Perry? Lady Gaga?

Nope. Someone more famous, more legendary than any of those ladies. My voice has been compared to that of the incomparable, the irrepressible, the unforgettable . . . Neil Young.

I know, I know—all of you are turning green with musical envy. And I understand, really I do. Why sing like a soft, pretty woman when you can croon like a caterwauling hillbilly?

Most folks don't say anything when I sing, no doubt struck speechless by my incredible vocal skills. My daughter is the only one who says she doesn't want to hear me. And I'm not sure why. When she was younger, I bought her a karaoke machine, and we sat on her bedroom floor, taking turns belting out songs by Sheryl Crow. Eventually, I bought her another microphone for the machine, and we sang songs together.

"You're a really good singer, Mommy," she said. Such a sweet little Neil Young fan.

Now a teenager, my daughter rolls her eyes and inserts earbuds at my slightest hum. And I have been instructed to NEVER sing in front of her friends.

Recently, I found myself driving my girl and her crew in our Honda SUV. I kept my mouth shut, trying not to do or say anything embarrassing, such as breathing.

She plugged her phone into the car stereo and began playing music from people with first names like "Lil" and last names like "Thug."

I willed myself deaf.

Although she's not allowed to listen to music with lots of bad words, I still hear shreds of phrases that gray my hair. Words that rhyme with "sick" and "duck." Words she shouldn't understand yet. Or ever.

It's a losing battle, because as she always says, "Mom, I ride the school bus. I know things."

Kill me now.

I certainly don't want to learn the lyrics to any of her music, and I'm just able to grasp words here and there. After a few minutes of listening to Lil Thug, I felt the need to shower, go to confession, maybe get a prescription for antibiotics.

But in the interest of peace, I remained quiet and willed my brain to its happy place. My inner jukebox played 70s soft rock, something long ago made into Muzak, something smacking of daisies and white gauzy dresses and orange sunsets.

What? You've never been mellow?

Right in the middle of my silent Olivia Newton-John

reverie, I almost didn't notice that Lil Thug abruptly stopped singing, and my girl queued up something different. Something kind of . . . awesome.

"I like big butts . . ."

My hips started wiggling, my head began bobbing. My daughter was playing *Baby Got Back* by Sir Mix-A-Lot, circa 1992, and she was enjoying it. From the corner of my eye, I saw her smile, saw her head-bob which was so much like mine.

But I dared not comment, and I knew I had better not sing. My role was the Silent Chauffeur. It was hard to contain myself, but I knew her rules. Thus, I had to be content with covert wiggle-dancing in my seat.

I looked in my rearview mirror at the girls in the backseat. They were loving the 20-plus-year-old song, all three of them bobbing, wiggling, singing. My daughter cranked the volume to speaker-blowing levels, and I bit my tongue as our Honda thumped and bounced down the road like a pimped-out Detroit Caddy.

And then, all of a sudden, it happened. The unthinkable. The unbelievable.

"Sing it, Mom! C'mon! You know every word!" said my daughter, excitement in her voice.

Glancing over to the passenger seat, I wondered: *Who was this child? Am I in the right car? Am I dreaming? Am I high?*

I couldn't quite believe my luck. Not only was I unbanned from singing, I was encouraged *to* sing. That hadn't happened in years. And she was right. Bad-ass gangsta that I am, I knew every word to the song.

As I began rapping, it struck me that the song had some teachable moments. "She gotta pack much back!"

It was clear that Mr. Mix-A-Lot appreciated a, um, round

female form. I hoped the girls were catching this. Apparently sexy women do eat food.

Kumbaya.

Though obviously chock-full of sage wisdom, Mr. Mix is no saint, as evidenced by some of the song's words. And I wasn't sure whether to sing one particular line, a sentence with questionable imagery. You know, the one where he compares a part of his anatomy to that of an anaconda. Then I remembered: *They listen to Lil Thug. They ride the school bus. They know things. Kill me now.*

So I belted out the line, loud and proud, followed by the second line, where the rapper wanted buns for his anaconda.

Laughter, smiles and giggles erupted. From girls. From teenagers. From my daughter. Hell hath surely frozen over in our Honda.

Clearly, I had made the right decision, throwing down that line. Maybe not a teachable moment, but a moment, nonetheless.

Not only that, but, for me, it was a lesson learned. As a mom of a teenage girl, I'll take that, any day.

Thank you, Sir Mix-A-Lot.

Dawn and daughter Laura

The Second Day of First Grade

by

Christy Lynne Williams

It was "Meet the Teacher Day" at my son's new school. I shuffled by desks and dodged other parents as my husband, Dan, and I followed our son Daniel in search of his desk.

"Doesn't this look like fun?" I asked, none too convincingly.

A stack of paperwork waited for us on Daniel's desk, listing many questions that we needed to answer. Filling out paperwork was a struggle because of the the roar of other parents and children, and I had to ask my first-grader for help. *How many students are they stuffing into this congested classroom?* I wondered.

I remembered Daniel's first day of kindergarten the previous year at the tiny Christian school. Every day, seven students and their parents lined up outside the classroom door. We greeted the teacher with a smile and said hello. Things were simple.

The information on this year's desk about bus routes, drop-off areas and crossing guards made my blood pressure rise. I wondered if Daniel's stomach felt as queasy as mine did.

Dan, Daniel and I looked around the room at the computers, calendars and charts then had our two minutes with Daniel's teacher, shaking hands and returning paperwork.

"I hope I'm not making a big mistake by sending him to this big public school," I said quietly to Dan as we left the classroom and headed to our car.

I spent the evening studying school manuals and pulling tags off items that we would donate to the classroom. Then, after a restless night, I rose before the sun, anxious for the day. Daniel happily dressed himself in his teal shirt and cargo pants, and, with a proud smile on his face, grabbed his superhero lunchbox.

"I will miss you while I'm at school," he said, trying to make me feel better.

"We will miss you, too," I said, choking back sobs.

I drove to school whispering every prayer I knew. Feeling lost, I followed the line of cars down the yellow-painted drop-off lane next to the sidewalk. *Should I park and walk him to his door? Can he find the classroom by himself?* But before I knew what was happening, I'd slowed to a stop and a chipper woman wearing an ID badge was opening my door and letting my baby out onto the curb.

"Do you know where you're headed?" she asked him.

"A2," Daniel replied, with confidence.

But does he even know where A2 is?! I wanted to scream in protest. I needed out. I needed to walk him to the door. But he was off like a rocket. I watched my heart bound through the gate toward the first-grade play area. The staff member closed my car door and waved me on. As my car crept forward, I craned my neck to see that his little teal shirt and superhero lunchbox were still heading in the right direction. *Should I get out and find him? But what good would that do?*

I drove away in tears, wondering if I'd get a phone call from the school saying that my child never showed up to class, that maybe "Stranger Danger" had hopped the gate and snatched him up minutes after I drove away. Perhaps a coyote had attacked him on the playground. Or maybe he'd found a lonely corner to curl up in and cry because his mom had just dropped him off at the curb.

Throughout the day, I checked my cellphone for messages as I counted down the minutes until dismissal. But at 2:15, I picked up a happy kid who was excited that his new friends liked his superhero lunch box.

Victorious, I started planning for the next great day. I created a "My Mom Loves Me" feast for his lunch, full of yogurt and little kabobs held together by sparkly cocktail stirrers. One held pieces of pepperoni, mozzarella chunks and olives and the other, raspberries, blueberries and strawberries. *This will be great!* I thought.

On the second day of first grade, I dropped Daniel off with a song in my heart and I looked forward to playing with our toddler while Daniel was at school. After school, I could hardly wait to hear about Daniel's super day. I didn't expect the little storm cloud that hopped into my car at 2:15.

"Don't ever pack me those cute lunches anymore," he fumed, wiping angry tears from his eyes.

"What?!" I felt as if I'd been hit from behind. "I did that because I love you. I thought you liked it when I did cute lunches!"

What uncharted territory have I stumbled into?

"The other kids made fun of me," he said, quivering. "They were all laughing at me."

"Laughing isn't always a bad thing. It doesn't always mean they don't . . ."

"It did," he interrupted. "They thought I was a baby."

Tears streamed down my cheeks as we drove home.

"I do like it when you do nice things like that," Daniel said. "I just don't want you to send things like that in my lunch anymore. Why do you want to make lunch hard? Why can't you make me a lunch like the other kids' lunches?"

I let go of a few things that day. I tried sorting out what was important and what wasn't, where to insist on originality and where to protect my child from unnecessary hurt.

The next morning, I arrived at the school feeling worse than I had the first day. My insecurity caused me to question the shirt he'd picked out and the crackers and cheese I'd packed. I thought about home schooling.

As we pulled close to the drop-off spot, I said, "I hope you have a really great day today, Daniel."

"Some days are good, and some days are bad." He shrugged. "That's just the way it is."

And from that day on, the enormous public school started feeling a little smaller, a little more comfortable to me.

"What about cutting your sandwich into a shape?" I asked Daniel one day, as I methodically packed yet another sandwich.

"Sure." Daniel shrugged, looking up from his homework.

"Really? I don't want you to get laughed at," I said, hesitating. "I just want to make it fun."

"I don't really care if they laugh," he said, to my surprise. "But I know they won't. They're my friends now."

And I knew he was right. Some days are bad, and some days are good. And this was a good day.

Left: Daniel on the first day of first grade.
Right: Christy Lynne holding Moses, with Daniel in front

Coupon Queen

by
Alice Muschany

My teenage daughters Julie and Jill made fun of my bargain shopping. If an item wasn't on sale, I refused to buy it. One Christmas, Julie handed me a large box wrapped in shiny paper and tied with red ribbons. Inside, I found several smaller boxes. The last one revealed my gift—a "Coupon Queen" button.

I wore it proudly.

When the holiday clearance sales began, I stormed down the aisles grabbing decorations, wrapping paper and bows. Hours later, arms loaded with bargains, I snuck in the back door and overheard my family discussing my shopping addiction.

"Mom's late. She probably found a super sale," Julie snickered.

Jill chimed in, "Geez. I hope it's something that fits now and not when it's out of style."

My husband, Roland, chided, "Girls, you know your

mother loves a bargain as much as an Arabian horse trader."

They all looked up as I slammed the door and rushed by with my loot. *I'll show them*, I steamed to myself. *My treasures will remain a secret.*

On another shopping trip, Bounty paper towels were half price. On top of that, I had 10 coupons. Who could pass that up? I bought them and snuck them home. When Roland spotted the rolls lined up in the cabinet like soldiers, he asked, "Are we getting a puppy?"

J. C. Penney's green-tag sale had entire racks marked down, plus I had an additional 15-percent-off coupon. Giddy, I rushed up and down the aisles, piling my cart high with deals.

Exhausted, I headed home. Bags rustled as I hurried past Roland to unload my stash. He followed me into the bedroom and watched as I pulled out three identical sweaters in different colors. Grinning, he teased, "Do we know someone with triplets?"

Jill walked in and giggled. "Mom's slipping. She forgot to buy one in pink."

Oh, I'll admit I've been burned a time or two. Once I used a fistful of coupons to purchase 20 containers of half-price yogurt. My funny man opened the fridge and said, "Eat up. Your yogurt expires in three days."

A few weeks later, the weatherman called for record-breaking snowfall, so I grabbed my coupons and rushed out to stock the shelves. Later that evening, Roland glanced in the pantry and said, "Wow! With all this food, we could absolutely survive a blizzard."

During a work break at my office the following Monday,

I opened a bag of tasty wheat crackers and ate one. I offered some to my co-worker. "Yum. These are delicious. Try one."

She helped herself to a cracker and took a bite. "They're really crisp. How much were they? Oh, never mind. You probably got them for nothing."

My reputation preceded me.

Not long after that, Roland searched the freezer for something to grill on the barbecue. When he didn't find anything, he opened the pantry door and noticed six boxes of cereal. "Let me guess," he said to me. "These were a steal. Too bad you didn't have a coupon for meat."

Last weekend, I rode along with Roland to Cabela's, the popular outdoor-recreation retailer. When he sat the waders on the counter and pulled out a coupon, I did a double take.

"Pardon me. Do I know you?" I asked him.

"Very funny. I just saved $20."

I called the girls immediately. "You're not going to believe who used a coupon." They chuckled when I told them.

After my daughters married, it didn't take them long to find out extra savings came in handy. While visiting Julie, I spotted a stack of coupons on her kitchen counter. Scooping them up, I asked, "Are these for me?"

She snatched the coupons out of my hand and said, "Not on my budget!"

Jill shocked me when she whipped out a coupon holder at the grocery store one day. *Praise the Lord! My frugal ways have rubbed off.*

Laughing, I said, "I can see us now. I'll trade you my Charmin coupon for your Tide."

My family has become such good bargain hunters that I worry this coupon queen might find herself dethroned. After one of their shopping sprees, the girls dropped by to show off their savvy bargains. Jill held up half-price bath towels from Kohl's. When I asked if she remembered to use the extra 20-percent-off coupon, her shoulders sagged. Julie bragged about the deal she'd found on a Mr. Coffee at Walmart.

Having studied the sale ads, I said smugly, "Too bad you didn't use the Target competitor ad. They advertised it $5 cheaper."

A huge smile spread across my face as I strutted away, proudly declaring, "Long live the Queen!"

Left to right: daughter Jill Hall, mom Alice Muschany and daughter Julie Smith

A Most Appropriate Moment

by
Liane Kupferberg Carter

"I have a girlfriend," my autistic son Mickey announced.

"You do?" I said. "Tell me about her."

"She doesn't talk much," he said. "She's shy."

I'd heard about her a few weeks earlier, when his teacher had emailed me about the friendship that was blossoming between Mickey and the girl in the classroom next door.

"Caroline goes on a daily walk on the bike path, and I have been letting Mickey go with her to offer encouragement—he quite enjoys this. I have to tell you that his mental demeanor is so improved when he gets that physical exercise. And it boosts his self-esteem, too, because he thinks he is helping Caroline."

Soon after, she emailed me this news:

"Just letting you know that Mickey asked his friend Caroline to the prom today. We will find out what color her dress is in case Mickey wants to get her a corsage."

"Oh, my. I think I need a tissue," I told my friend.

"Are you kidding? I'd need a whole box," she said. "This is a monumental milestone moment."

I phoned the florist. The afternoon before the prom, I took Mickey to the shop. With a big smile, the florist produced a small white box. Carefully, the man peeled back layers of tissue paper to reveal a wrist corsage of rosebuds and ribbons nestled within. Mickey peered at it silently.

"She'll love it," the florist assured him.

Mickey nodded. All business, he pulled out his wallet. "How much does it cost?"

"Thirty-five dollars."

Mickey placed two $20 bills on the counter. He remembered to wait for his change. Then, as we walked back to the car, he confided to me, "I hugged Caroline today."

"You did? What did she say?"

"She said, 'I love you.'"

"Really," I said, feigning nonchalance. "And what did you say?"

"I said, 'I love you, too.'"

Oh my, I thought.

The prom took place in the school's gym. Students were decked out in their party best. Parents were invited, too. "But we shouldn't hover," I reminded my husband, Marc. It was a reminder to me, as well.

We watched from the sidelines as Mickey and Caroline clasped hands. Together, they jumped up and down, with looks of sheer joy on both their faces. Each time he took her by one hand and twirled her around, teachers and staff applauded. Marc and I *kvelled*—a Yiddish word that means "to burst with pride and pleasure for one's child." It's related to the German word *quellen*, which means "to well up."

Which I confess I was also doing. A lot.

Because here's the thing: I never expected him to go to a prom. Prom was one of so many things in the litany of what we were told he would never be able to do. He would never be social. Never have empathy. Would always prefer solitude.

Why do professionals persist in telling these things to parents? Especially when it was clear, even from the earliest days, that our son liked—in fact, craved—connection?

Yet here he was, at a prom. With a date. Maybe "prom" didn't look the way I thought prom would look, but this wasn't about me. It was time for me to let go of any lingering regret for what wasn't and to accept what was right in front of us. This was still a prom. His prom.

And Mickey was incandescent.

Mickey and Caroline jumped and twirled for 45 minutes before Mickey finally joined us to announce, "I've had enough."

"You need to tell Caroline," I told him. I watched him return to her side. He hugged her gently. Started back toward us. Stopped. Turned. Hugged her tenderly once more.

When he returned, he asked his dad, "Was that appropriate?"

A lump-in-the-throat moment. That he felt he had to ask . . . well, of course. Because for most of his life, he's had teachers and therapists and parents guiding him on what is appropriate and inappropriate behavior.

Appropriate?

Was it ever.

Liane and son Mickey

Rules

by
Lisa McManus Lange

There is another side to my mother-self—the inner teen rebel who yearns to break the odd little rule, just because.

The good mother I try to be hides this other side of me, enforcing the rules by way of not-so-lengthy lectures and leading by example. But some rules confine me and urge me to break free. The saying "Rules are made for a reason" often grates on my nerves, but "Rules are meant to be broken" makes up for it.

A few exotic creatures who attempted to find their way into our lives quickly changed my attitude toward rules that are made for a reason. Specifically, rules made by landlords:

"Don't hang this, don't paint that." Party pooper.

"No noise after such-and-such time." Personally, I love that one.

"No dogs allowed." Not a favorite.

With two kids in our back pocket, homelessness is not an option. We are renters, and therefore we follow the rules and stick to acceptable animal companions such as one fish and one cat. I would give *anything* to smuggle in a non-barking, non-shedding, non-peeing teeny-tiny dog that no one could *possibly* ever notice. But for silly reasons like setting a good example for our children and avoiding eviction, my husband and I refrain from smuggling in anything of the canine persuasion.

Our children learned to negotiate early in life: "If we can't have a dog, can we have a . . ." Of course, nothing simple like adding a hamster was ever entertained. As my darling boys approached their preteen and teenage years, their desire for the exotic increased daily. Tarantulas, scorpions and weird bugs only found on the vines in the Amazon were on their wish list. Dreams of fame and notoriety on the playground fueled their desire. Plans such as, "When my fish dies, can I get a squid?" were always in the making.

A trip to the local zoo was supposed to be a family bonding experience. If I had thought long and hard about it, I would have steered clear of the place. Geared for all ages (but not the squeamish), the aptly named "Bug Zoo" in Victoria, British Columbia, showcases critters found only in jungles afar. Much to my chagrin, signs posted at a perfect 5-foot-tall viewing height advertised various little creatures "FOR SALE." Scorpions and praying mantises were up for grabs, but nothing tame like ants or dew worms. And, of course, the excited voices from my own brood broke through the incessant chirping of the crickets: "Look, Mom, they're cheaper here than at the pet store!"

My mind scurried like cockroaches at the bottom of the cage. *How do they know the prices at the pet store?* I asked myself.

Much later, our home was a beehive of activity. Excitement, research and planning for the scorpions and praying mantises we apparently were going to house were forefront. Names were lovingly chosen.

As the only parent not "into the whole thing," I tried everything to diffuse the excitement. I ranted that with a time-consuming, most-demanding cat, I would *not* be catering to a scorpion/praying mantis/whatever, as well. I argued that I could barely afford to feed my family, never mind a bug.

And I pleaded for my children's lives; no creature was worth the deadly risk of a poisonous bite . . . even though I threaten their lives daily at the sight of dirty dishes in the sink. I came up with every imaginable reason why only trained professionals should handle these creatures. But common knowledge prevailed—as a mother, I knew absolutely nothing.

I am not afraid of these caged darlings, but I felt that my boys, aged 9 and 13 at the time, were not yet responsible enough to handle such exotic species. *Whatever happened to simple ant farms?* I wondered.

In the middle of the excitement, after the piggy bank had been smashed and the pennies duly counted, my husband had a flash of brilliance. He realized he should check the tenancy rules regarding exotic pets. The darling landlord, who many love to hate, listed all the specimens not allowed—tarantulas, scorpions, praying mantises. And, much to my glee, here's why:

1) Escapees could kill the neighbors.
2) Uncontrollable population growth of said escapees would lead to costly extermination.

3) Chirping crickets, often escapees themselves to avoid becoming menu options, keep the neighbors awake at night.

So that settled that. No exotic pets.

As I breathed a sigh of relief, I truly believed I was likely the only tenant who wanted to smooch the landlord in gratitude. Our lives had been saved.

My heart went out to the boys as I broke the news. Their tears washed away their hopes that had risen higher than any anthill. But they slowly became resigned to the fact that this is the way of the renter's life—landlords and rules.

Thanks to our landlord, not only did I not have to be the bad guy, but I also wouldn't be bugged daily by scorpions and other creepy-crawly pets. I came to love rules, my landlord and, quite possibly, the cat just a little more.

A Bucket Full

by
Pamela Frost

I would never have chosen to be a single mom, but stuff happens. I tried to make the best of it and provide my son with activities he might have otherwise engaged in with a father. Living in a cottage on Chippewa Lake in Ohio, fishing was one of our favorite activities.

Each spring our little village sponsored a fishing derby and Chris was anxious to show off his skills as an angler. He hurried down the street to the lake, carrying his orange tackle box in one hand and his kid-sized Zebco rod and reel in the other. He walked well ahead of me, as seven year olds do, not wanting to be seen with his mother.

I stood proudly behind Chris as he signed up without my help for the children's division.

Councilman Fred looked at me and said, "Aren't you signing up, too?"

I laughed. "Really?" I waved a hand at the docks. "Like I

stand a chance against those guys with their fancy bass boats and their fish finders. Them's some serious bass fishermen."

"Top prize goes to the person with the most total weight," he explained.

The gears began to turn in my head. I remembered being on my friend's boat while he cast his spinner baits repeatedly in search of Mr. Big Daddy Bass and came up empty. Meanwhile, I was hauling in bluegill all day with my bobber and worm.

Giving a sheepish little smile, I slid my hand down into my jean pocket and fished out money for my entry fee. I ran back up to the house to get my gear.

At 2 P.M., my son and I were standing with all the other fishermen on the beach waiting for the signal to begin. Everyone scattered at the sound of the horn. A couple of macho guys jumped into their bass boats and went roaring away from the beach, putting on quite a show in the process.

Chris and I strolled to our favorite spot in the outlet. I knew the bluegill would be plentiful since I'd seen them spawning there earlier in the spring when the lake level was down.

I threaded a piece of night crawler onto Chris's hook and he plopped his bobber into a perfect spot. I got my pole rigged up, and as soon as my bobber hit the water, Chris was standing next to me dangling a naked hook. I pulled another slimy critter from the cup and soon he was fishing again.

I reeled in a nice palm-sized bluegill and dropped it into my waiting drywall bucket. As soon as my bobber hit the water, Chris shouted, "I got one!" I took his fish off the hook and dropped it into his bucket. He didn't like to get his hands dirty. I worried that I was raising a prissy boy, but only for a moment, as I had fishing to do. I baited him up again and sent him on his way.

I watched my bobber for about a whole minute when Chris yelled, "It's stuck!" His bobber was hanging from a tree, which was not an unusual occurrence. I sighed, gave my pole a parting glance and went to the rescue.

Once done, I hurried back to my spot. Looking at my watch, I saw we had already burned quite a bit of time and I had only one fish. Chris had only one fish. I gave some serious thought to throwing my fish in his bucket. But that would be cheating, and what kind of message would that send to my kid? I argued with myself that it was just one little fish. I wanted him to win the kids' division.

I'm not proud to admit it, but I really wanted to win the adult prize—to show all those macho fishermen I could do it, and to make my son proud of me. Taking a quick sideways glance at Chris, I saw he was happily yo-yoing his bobber in and out of the water. I made the decision right then and there to get serious about catching lots of fish.

The fish began cooperating quite nicely. About the time my bobber hit the water, I had a nibble. There were quite a few fish in the bucket when Chris approached with his naked hook.

I handed him the cup-o-worms. "Here, you do it," I said, not taking my eyes off my bobber.

"Gross! They're all slimy."

"Rules say you gotta bait your own hook," I lied. He found a stick and fished out a fat night crawler then carried it back to his spot, the worm dangling from the stick.

I returned to some serious fishing. I called into question my parenting skills and figured I'd probably fry in hell for this, but I fished on. I pulled in a few more nice-sized fish.

Sparing a quick look down the bank to check on Chris, I noticed he had laid the worm on a rock and was chasing it around, trying to poke the hook into it without touching the worm. This made me laugh. Good Mommy wanted to come to the rescue and bait his hook for him again, but Competitive Pam saw the bobber go down and began fishing for the money again. In my defense, I was not being totally irresponsible—I did have one watchful "mommy ear" cocked for the sound of my kid falling into the water. But aside from that, I was fishing. I was in the moment with the fish. My pole and I were one. The bluegills were giving me a great run.

Chris was having no luck getting the worm to crawl voluntarily onto his hook. He came to me whining, "I don't want to fish anymore."

He looked quite surprised when I said, "OK, go to the playground." I could see the swings from where I sat fishing and was comfortable with that. Our little village was a place where everybody looked out for all the kids.

When the horn blew, signaling the end of the derby, Chris ran to me and looked in the bucket. "Wow, Mom, that's a lot of fish. I bet you'll win."

"I don't know about that," I said laughing, tousling his blond hair. I had the drywall bucket nearly full of fish. *But would it be enough?* I thought.

I had trouble carrying the bucket to the weigh-in. Men

stood on the beach with their stringers of bass and northern pike, proud of their beautiful fish. I felt a little intimidated.

Finally, it was my turn. Chuckles rippled through the crowd as I dragged the bucket up to the scales. No one seemed to take me seriously.

The official looked in my bucket, at the spectators and fellow fishermen then rolled his eyes. "Well, let's humor the little lady," he said aloud, with a shrug. He then began to throw my fish onto the scale.

It became very quiet as the needle climbed. To everyone's surprise, the needle came to the same point as the leader's catch, and I still had two fish in the bucket. Chris clapped and jumped up and down, yelling, "My mom won!"

So maybe I wasn't such a bad mom after all, even though I still felt guilty for not helping my son win. But it's important for a kid to be proud of his mom, isn't it? To feel better about my mothering skills, I took Chris and his friends to Chuck E. Cheese's pizza with the prize money . . . and no, I didn't play the kid's fishing arcade game.

Ma's in the Cupboard

by
Cynthia Ballard Borris

"Keep looking, guys." I dragged another wooden drawer from the kitchen and dumped the contents onto the living room floor. "They've got to be in here somewhere."

I sifted through the pile of crinkled napkins, loose marbles and faded photographs.

My son Karl hauled out a second drawer. The weight rested on his thighs. "Where do you want this one?"

"No, not there. We've already gone through that stuff." I flung my hand to a vacant spot on the littered carpet. "Over there."

With a shift to the left, he lifted the rectangular box and started to pour. Papers fluttered to the ground, covering the last naked spot.

"OK, everyone! Hit the ground and start searching." I crawled on all fours, shuffling through 20 years of junk and treasures. My youngest son, Grant, turned a third drawer upside down, and trinkets cascaded to the carpet.

"What are we looking for?" Questioning stares came from my three kids.

"Recipes," I answered.

"Recipes?" they echoed.

"I hear recipes are a big hit on the Internet." The words flowed. "All I have to do is post my favorite recipes, and we'll be rich."

A tremor of shock rattled the room, a bottle of antacids rolled out of the cupboard and the kids gulped in unison. Unfettered, I pushed the non-supportive threesome aside, sliding my hands into the collection. This was business.

I studied an ancient piece of paper, the ink drawn and faded. Beyond the missing directions, I smelled possibility. I folded it and tucked the paper into my back pocket.

Karl held a tube of tub caulking and a bicycle pump. "I thought this was a kitchen drawer."

"It is." I nodded and pushed a plastic ant out of my way.

"Whoa! Look what I found." Erin cradled a toy ice cube with a fly in the center.

"Recipes, guys, recipes . . ." I tossed a handful of expired coupons into the fire in our fireplace. "Everyone else is making all the money. This is serious."

Voices still, fingers filed childhood souvenirs into stacks while discarding non-qualifiers to the trash. A tiny bug escaped from the dusty drifts. Erin found a party horn in the mess and tooted a sour squeal.

"Remember when Mom put peas in the guacamole

instead of avocado and thought no one would notice her fat-free pea dip?" Karl said as he separated items.

"All right, that one bombed, but how about . . ." I prepared to make my case.

Grant upped the prosecution's memory bank. "Yeah, how about when Mom gave her friend the strawberry smoothie, high in protein, and it exploded all over his office."

"It wasn't my fault it fermented," I protested.

"Or the day she lost the football bet and made the same guy a sandwich with the plastic cheese." Laughter exploded and the lamps rocked. "And he had a lunchtime meeting, so he gave the sandwich to his boss."

"So that one backfired, but he was the one who gave the sandwich away, not me," I reminded the gang.

That was a good one, I chuckled to myself. Cheese stamped "Made in China." Even now, the post-lunchtime call, "Lucy, you have some 'splaining . . ." tickles my memory.

"Is this guy still your friend, Mom?" Erin finger-counted the mishaps.

"The best of." I looked at her and winked.

Nonstop, my sons and daughter tallied Mom's "mis-culinary" moments. I intensified the scavenger hunt. Kids or not, I wouldn't be derailed.

Karl drew deep into his childhood and pulled out a winner. "One year, she took us camping and forgot the food."

"That doesn't count. How many years ago was that? Eight? Nine? That has nothing to do with my cooking talents." I shoved a magnet covered with 2-inch nails, some Christmas ornament hangers and a couple of picture hangers into the discard corner.

Still, no recipe of worth.

"That was the same year she melted the sleeping bag," Grant said, wiping streaks of tears from his flushed face, "and screamed there was a bear in the tent." The scrapbook of haunts flipped another page. The room burst with ghosts best left to childhood memories.

"All right, so I'm not perfect." Slowly, I sorted and shifted through miscellaneous debris on the floor. "I didn't scream. I loudly suggested." I cleared my throat in an attempt to regain my Mom status. *Dang raccoon; felt like a bear.*

Refocused, the mom-bashing eased and we continued to rummage for recipes that would lead to wealth.

Soon, Karl held a tattered paper. Grease spots scalloped the edges. "Look, Mom's killer Boston cream pie recipe."

"My secret recipe!" I reached through the air for the list of ingredients. Step by step, every word was clear and legible. *Finally, I can post something.* I felt my pocketbook expanding with anticipation.

"Isn't that the one that sent Grandpa to the hospital?" Erin asked.

Stone faces stared at the paper. The room fell silent.

"Poor Grandpa," Grant said. A whisper of empathy christened his lips.

I flopped back onto the floor, and a thumbtack stabbed the palm of my hand. A tiny Smurf figurine smiled from the mess. I didn't smile back.

"Maybe you should stick to writing football stories and bunny tales, Ma," Karl said.

Ma? Just when did I go from Mommy to Ma? I wondered.

Strong arms wrapped around my neck. A hug sealed the question, and we tossed the tainted recipe into the fire. With a crackle and a pop, my secret concoction succumbed to ash, and I conceded the recipe battle to the cuisine experts.

Left to right: daughter Erin, Mom AKA Cynthia, sons Grant and Karl (the tall one in the back), vintage 1992.

Measuring Up

by
Dahlynn McKowen

Moms. We are always on the go, go, go and many times, ignore ourselves in the process.

I used to be one of those busy moms. Back in the day, I held a full-time, high-level management position which ran me ragged. Up early, kids off to school, commute to work to earn my very, very nice paycheck. When it was time to head home, my day went in reverse. Commute, pick up the kids from after-school care then prepare dinner and help with homework. I nary had a moment for myself, except for an occasional glass of wine after the kids were tucked in.

To top everything off, perimenopause was beginning to frustrate me to no end. From sagging body parts to fledging chin hairs, from fading eyesight to a fading memory, I tried my best to ignore all the signs. I also tried my best to ignore the fact that daily exercise and eating right were not a part of my normal routine. Getting used to this phase of my life at age

43 was slowly becoming a reality. But no one could make this fact more evident to me than my then 10-year-old son Shawn.

From the day he was born, Shawn had always been on the small side. To keep up his self-esteem, the family made it a point to praise him for growing taller, using everyday household objects to gauge his growth. From the first time Shawn was able to see in the bathroom mirror by himself without having to use a stool to being able to sit at the family dinner table without the help of a telephone book, growth milestones in Shawn's life were a constant in our home.

A favorite growth milestone for Shawn was the kitchen countertop. He loved cooking with me, but had to stand on a stool to help. Shawn dreamed of the day he wouldn't have to use the stool anymore to flip pancakes or operate the hand-held mixer.

Then the day came—Shawn finally grew tall enough to see over the counter, and the stool was retired. It was then I realized I had to come up with yet another new growth milestone. Looking around, the next obvious one was the top of the refrigerator—at 5-foot 7-inches tall, *I* couldn't even see over the top of this large appliance. Stumped, I decided to compare my darling son's height to mine, and to use my boobs as his new growth milestone.

My favorite thing in the world is to get hugs from my boy, who is lovable, caring and compassionate. Upon setting the new milestone, whenever he would hug me, I'd say, "Oh, Shawn! You're almost as tall as my *boobs!*" He'd giggle, mainly because I would over enunciate the word "boobs."

One morning, when I was enjoying my wake-up hug from

Shawn, I was shocked over how tall he was, compared with my boobs. It was as if he had grown 4 inches overnight!

"Shawn, look how tall you are! You're taller than my *boobs*!" I exclaimed, mid-hug.

Shawn pulled away and looked up at me with sleepy eyes. He mumbled, "Duh, Mom. You're not wearing a bra." He then headed into the living room to watch TV.

I stood in the kitchen, dumbfounded. Looking down at my perimenopausal body, I realized that Shawn hadn't grown 4 inches overnight, but quite the opposite—my boobs had decided to sag 4 inches.

Thanks to my loving, compassionate, caring and *honest* 10-year-old, I had a breast reduction and lift the following year. Now Shawn is 17 and way taller than my new boobs, and I wouldn't have it any other way.

Shawn and Dahlynn, 2007

CHAPTER EIGHT

Letting Go

You did your best.

Learning to Fly

by
Georgia Hubley

A tinge of fear and a shiver ran through me as I stared at the red-circled date on my calendar. Inside the circle were two words emblazoned in capital letters: MOVING DAY. My life would change drastically in exactly two weeks because my husband and I had sold our home of almost 20 years and were moving into a condo. It would be just the two of us.

My husband had an exciting job and felt fulfilled. But I had retired a month earlier, due to a large conglomerate gobbling up my employer of almost two decades. What was I going to do with my life?

It was not easy sorting through old keepsakes and deciding what we'd hold onto and what we'd donate to a charitable organization. Time was slipping by too quickly, and I felt overwhelmed by what was left to do.

The garage was my husband's domain, but I remembered I had a few things stored there, too. I scanned the rafters above and spotted a big, black bag tucked away in plastic. I climbed the ladder and tossed the bag down to the garage floor. I removed the plastic and eased myself down to sit in the old chair one last time. It had been years since the beanbag chair had sat in our son Nick's bedroom. My chest tightened. I felt a slight tug, and my heart ached a little. As I held my head in my hands and tried to choke back the tears, my mind swirled with memories.

My first inkling of our only child's wild imagination came when Nick was three-and-a-half—he was enthralled with the movie *The Wizard of Oz*. After watching his first television broadcast of the show, he ran into the kitchen while straddling my new broom. He gulped for air between sobs and whined, "The broom won't fly. The broom won't fly."

I could barely contain my laughter, but somehow I did. It took a while to console him, but he accepted my explanation that flying on a broom was only make-believe.

However, Nick's imagination soared. After watching a production of *Peter Pan*, he obsessed over the elfin-like boy who loved to fly and refused to grow up.

"Mommy, I'm not sleepy," Nick said, as I tucked him in that night. "When I close my eyes, I can see myself flying across the sky." I kissed his forehead and assured him he'd fall asleep soon.

The next morning, I was awakened by a loud thud. Immediately, I raced to Nick's bedroom.

"I learned to fly!" he announced.

He'd leaped from his top bunk bed into the black beanbag chair, splitting the seam I'd recently repaired. There he sat, covered with hundreds of tiny, white foam beans, grinning sheepishly, his cheeks flushed, the thrill of success making his blue eyes even brighter than usual.

That incident ended his interest in physically learning to fly, but it didn't deter his passion for musical theater—a passion that continued to evolve from kindergarten through high school. During his first year of college, Nick was offered a role in a national touring company of *A Chorus Line*. He asked us if he could choose to perform instead of finishing college.

"Pursue your dream. Go for it." We gave our blessings and proudly watched his career flourish.

Our nest was empty much sooner than we'd planned. To ease our anguish, during the week, we focused on our jobs. As often as possible, we took weekend getaways and watched Nick perform.

Suddenly, the garage door opened, thrusting me back to reality.

"Surprise!" Nick shouted. "I have a couple of days off from the show. Thought you could use my help—I can help you pack."

"Oh, I am glad you came!" I said. "It is going to be difficult for me to part with this old beanbag chair. Would you like to sit in it one more time?"

He plopped his lanky frame next to me, and we laughed as the patched seam gave way. Foam beans escaped, some flying about, others spilling forth onto the garage floor.

"Just like old times," Nick said. "Don't worry—I'll clean up the mess and toss the chair in the dumpster."

Relieved, I leaned over and gave him a quick hug. I confided

I was engulfed with memories that I would like to share. I told Nick that I wanted to write full time in my retirement. "But I'm afraid to give it a try," I said.

"Mom, you always gave me free reign to indulge my imagination and my dreams to reach my goals. Now it's my turn to support you. Go for it!"

That was 13 years ago. Since then, I have learned that an empty nest is the perfect place for a mom to spread her wings. I, too, have learned to fly.

Georgia and son Nick at the San Francisco airport, waiting for him to board a plane for New York City to pursue his acting career, circa 1983.

Empty House

by
Mary Laufer

I awoke to the sound of water rushing in the shower. For no discernible reason, my teenage daughter was up before dawn—again. I squinted to see the clock and saw it glowing the red numerals "4:40." Ugh! I sank back into my pillow.

"One more week," I whispered. "Emily will be off to college."

For the first time in my life, I was going to be alone. My son had married in June, and then my husband was temporarily transferred out of state. Now my daughter planned to attend a local university and live in the dormitory. This fall, I would not only have an empty nest, but an empty house.

The cat tiptoed over the bedspread, stuck her whiskers in my face and purred. I turned over and tried to go back to sleep, but then a hair dryer buzzed. It was no use.

When I walked into the hallway, I almost tripped over a

pile of Emily's Care Bears. "You don't want these anymore?" I asked her from outside the bathroom door.

"No," Emily said. "You can give them away."

I picked up the stuffed animals and threw them into a box in my closet. It was already full of her old books, purses and jewelry. Emily didn't talk much about leaving home, but I got the feeling I wasn't the only one counting down the days.

After breakfast, I tried to work at my computer while music blasted. "Can you turn down the radio?!" I yelled.

Emily lowered the volume slightly. I shook my head. "One more week."

Move-in day at the college finally came. A woman behind a desk handed Emily a key, and she eagerly grabbed it and grinned. When I headed toward the elevator with her, she hesitated. "Mom, I don't want you to come up with me."

Another parent might have insisted, but I saw this as a step toward independence and allowed my daughter to move into the dorm herself.

My first morning alone, I awoke in daylight and sighed. I looked forward to working in peace and quiet. But when I sat in front of my computer, I couldn't concentrate. Something was missing. I turned on some music—yes, that was it. I remembered that when Emily had gone to preschool, I had turned on cartoons for background noise.

At 3:15, a school bus rumbled down the street and squeaked to a stop next door. I suddenly felt very old. The school years that had passed so slowly now seemed to have gone by very quickly.

The next time I looked up from the computer screen,

it was 6:30 and dark outside. When my family had been home, I'd started dinner around 4:30 and we had eaten together at 6 o'clock. Every night, I'd served a balanced meal, something different, something we all liked. Now I went to the kitchen and pulled out the frying pan. I scrambled two eggs and tossed in some leftover broccoli.

When I sat down at the kitchen table, the cat rubbed against my leg. "You miss her, too, don't you, Midnight?"

My daughter had pampered her black cat for years. Now she had nothing to do with her. The animal jumped into my lap, and I petted her soft ears. When the phone rang, she hopped down.

"So how do you like being alone?" my husband asked.

"I can see why people who live by themselves have pets," I said.

He laughed. "Are you going to end up one of those old cat ladies?"

"I hope not!"

In the days that followed, I immersed myself in work, staying up until 1 A.M. and sleeping in each morning. There was no child to keep me on a schedule.

I hadn't heard from Emily in more than two weeks, so I phoned the dorm. Her roommate assured me that my daughter was still alive, but Em refused to return my calls. I was mortified. *Has she discarded me like she has her Care Bears?* I worried. *Has she disowned me along with the cat?* I'd been ready to let her go, but not like this. I walked aimlessly through the house, a hollow feeling growing inside me.

The days became colder, and leaves fell from the trees.

During the last week in October, my neighbors put up Halloween decorations, and I wondered if I should, too. I'd never been alone before on Halloween. Maybe I'd turn out the lights and go to a movie.

I paged through our old photo albums and looked at pictures taken on other Halloweens—my son as a Smurf, my daughter as a princess. I thought of all the older people who gave treats to my kids over the years, even if they had no children at home.

On Halloween day, a key turning in the deadbolt startled me. Emily came in and set down her backpack. Without saying hello she asked, "Did you get candy?"

"Two big bags," I said, catching my breath.

"Can I hand it out?"

"Sure."

My daughter disappeared to her bedroom. When the doorbell rang, she swished down the stairs in her long pink prom dress from last spring. She clicked across the floor in high heels, looking like an older version of the princess she had been at age six.

Emily grabbed the bowl of candy and opened the door. Two boys dressed as vampires yelled, "Trick or treat!" and she dropped chocolate bars into their bags. Midnight sat on the windowsill and hissed at them. It was as if the clock had been turned back a few years.

Before Emily went to bed, she told me she wanted to move back home and take the light-rail train to her classes. She didn't offer a reason. Undoubtedly, dorm life wasn't what she had thought it would be, just as empty nest wasn't what I expected.

Early the next morning, I heard the sound of rushing water in the shower and smiled. It was a good sound. No, it was a *wonderful* sound.

Top: Emily and mom Mary
Right: Emily in her prom dress

No Trampoline Tonight

by
Laurel McHargue

I suppose it's a good thing that my goal is to live to be 110 because after spending the last several hours cleaning my son's apartment, I may inadvertently have sacrificed a year or two.

He didn't ask me to do it, and he certainly didn't expect that I would. We were supposed to enjoy a merry old time with a group of his friends who had invited us for dinner and then an evening at the local indoor trampoline park. Awesome, right? Yes, I was ready to don a set of Nick's sweats and hop till I dropped, but an unexpected call from his workplace changed our plans, leaving me with four hours to entertain myself, and no cable television.

"I guess I'll have some time to write after all," I told him as he hurriedly dressed to cover a co-worker's shift. He looked great in his dress pants, shirt and tie, but cut himself in his rush to shave.

"Why are you using a disposable razor?" I asked, knowing from personal experience how unforgiving they can be.

"I don't know," he said, pressing a piece of toilet paper to his chin. "A leftover habit from when I didn't used to shave every day, I guess."

If he could, he'd likely never shave, but his job now required it. I made a mental note to buy him a real razor.

He left, and I opened the refrigerator to rustle up some dinner. Looked like it would be a celery-and-peanut-butter extravaganza, and when I opened what should have been the fruit drawer to see if there was anything I might add to my meal, I recoiled in horror.

No, there wasn't a severed head or any other body part in the drawer, but there was clearly something growing, and not something anyone should eat. I decided that my young bachelor could use a little help and set aside the celery for later.

I surveyed the small apartment and decided to start with the drab beige-brown linoleum that almost hid months of neglect. After running the vac (note: buy new vacuum bags), I filled the tub with bleach water and searched for a mop, but found only a dry-mop. Into the tub it went, and I instantly felt better slopping it across each room and capturing all the dust bunnies.

The color of the tub water when I rinsed the mop made me think that I should repeat what I'd just done, several times, but my time was limited, and there was much still to do—like clean the tub, which bloomed both black and an unnatural pink; and the toilet, which rocked when you sat on it; and the sink, which is attached to the wall at the perfect height for a Lilliputian.

I looked for a new sponge (note: buy new sponges), to no avail, so I used the one that keeps the bar of soap from slipping into the sink; it was in considerably better shape than the scary one Nick has been using on dishes in the kitchen. My hands started to look like old lady's hands (I've only just hit my middle-age) and I wondered if I should have worn a hazmat mask, but it was too late. I'd gone too far.

After dousing all bathroom surfaces with bleach (note: buy more bleach), I scrubbed what I could, including the abused trash can. Then I went back to the kitchen. I opened the refrigerator again, hoping that what I had seen an hour ago wasn't really as bad as I had first thought, but, in fact, it was far worse.

When I removed the drawer to clean it in the sink, what I found under it at the bottom of the refrigerator defied description, and for a moment, I considered pretending I'd not seen it. I could have cleaned and replaced the drawer, and no one would have been the wiser. But then I wouldn't have been able to sleep. Ever.

And so I did what I must with a skanky sponge soaked in antibacterial spray (note: buy more antibacterial spray), and as the saying goes, one thing led to another. I did my best not to breathe each time I went in for a scrub, but I started to hear what the doctors' dialogue might be when I'm 108.

"Poor old girl," they might say. "I'll bet she cleaned her son's refrigerator when she was just middle-aged. There's no way she'll make it to 110 now."

Nevertheless, I knew that I would finish what I'd begun.

When all of the red-green gooey jelly-like substance was gone, I finished up by scraping a meal's worth of food from the inside of the microwave and wiped down the stove front and hood. The sponge could handle no more, and my peanut butter celery was calling me.

I cleaned the kitchen trashcan, tossed in the mangled sponge, and scrubbed my flaky hands with the last drop of antibacterial spray. It was time for dinner (note: buy more celery) and three—yes, three—brownies. Hey, I now knew that I was only going to live to be 108, so I figured I might as well enjoy every moment!

Nick returned shortly after 10 P.M. and I noted a brief expression of concern on his face. He sensed that something was different but couldn't put his finger on it.

"Wow. I normally just carry the whole trashcan to the dumpster. You were brave to pull out that flimsy bag," he told me when he saw the over-full bag by the front door.

I told him just how brave I had been.

"Thanks, Mum," he told me, and I knew that we would both sleep well that night.

Letting go has not been easy, but I have discovered that even though my son may not prioritize things in his life as I have in mine, he ultimately will be OK. And so will I.

The ABCs of ACTs

by
Ellie Grossman

In an effort to help my son achieve academic success (aka, get into a decent college), I decided to do my part without being overly involved.

Now this can be a tightrope act for moms. As a parent of a high-school junior, I felt overwhelmed just thinking about the near future. Somehow, Jack had to maintain a high GPA, stay involved in his activities, get a job, study for the PSAT, SAT and ACT, schedule campus tours and fill out college applications. But, most importantly, Jack had to learn how to operate a washing machine so that when he left home the following year, he wouldn't have to wear the same smelly T-shirt every day and offend his roommate and accounting professor.

Most moms know the correlation between good grades and a peaceful home environment. But since that was not going to happen, I decided to do something more tangible to help Jack prepare for the road ahead. The first step was for him to sharpen his pencils and his mind for the upcoming ACTs. Since I'm not an algebra or chemistry wiz, I was on a mission to expand my son's vocabulary. I began to collect ACT words in the same way I used to scavenge for seashells on the beach when he was a little kid.

I printed out high-frequency academic vocabulary words, from "acute" to "disparage," on separate pieces of paper and arranged them—alphabetically, of course—in a three-prong, two-pocket folder. Each word was bold-faced with a definition and example sentence to further my son's understanding. I even labeled the blue plastic cover "ACT 2012" with a thick, black Sharpie.

When I eagerly showed Jack the project I had diligently worked on during the two-hour season premiere of *American Idol*, he didn't seem impressed or appreciative. In fact, his exact words were, "You're wasting your time." This hurt my feelings. Nevertheless, I was determined to do my job as a good mom.

Fortunately, Jack was enrolled at the "ACT School of Missouri"—at least that's what the principal called it—and the teachers were required to bombard students with new words every day to increase their test scores. In the school newsletter, it said, "Research shows that the size of a student's vocabulary is one of the most important language-related factors for achievement in education. Therefore, our goal for this semester is to introduce students to 20 new words each month." Words like "apocryphal" and "circumspect" were featured on the school's website, announced over the intercom and posted throughout the school's hallways, classrooms and cafeteria. And I would hazard to guess the words were probably displayed in the bathrooms, as well, although I was afraid to go in and check.

I decided to do my part by sneaking these words into our daily family conversations. For example:

"I'm not sure what to make for dinner tonight, since I'm an *abstract* thinker."

"Don't hurt your sister's feelings with your *caustic* remarks about her homework."

"There seems to be a *dearth* of food in the refrigerator, so I'd better go to the grocery store."

"Watch your mouth, young man. You should strongly *censor* your cursing."

"Your father is *meshugge* for bowling 10 games in a row." (Can't hurt to throw in a little Yiddish vocabulary, as well.)

Finally, whether he was ready or not, the day came for Jack to take the standardized ACT test at the nearby high school. Unfortunately, it was the crack of dawn, and for a boy who does not normally wake up until lunchtime, the odds were against him before he scribbled in his first tiny bubble on the test form.

On his way out the door, I made sure Jack had plenty of sharpened #2 pencils and an extra Texas Instruments calculator in case the batteries died in his other one. I also gave him strawberry-flavored Jolly Rancher hard candy, hoping the sugar would prevent him from dozing off. I felt like I was sending my kid to science camp.

Five hours later, when the students were dismissed from the test, I waited for Jack in the parking lot. He opened the front passenger door of our van and dropped his exhausted body into the seat as if he had just finished playing a double-header baseball game, only without the dirt on his pants.

I asked Jack how it went. He responded sarcastically with his ACT words, "I *disdain* school. I *scrutinized* every question. Now I'm *parched*. Let's go get a smoothie."

I could not be more proud.

Ellie congratulating son Jack following his 2013
high school graduation

So Long to Superheroes

by
Dianna Graveman

I am not a shopper. I like having new things as much as the next person. I just don't like cruising for parking spaces, standing in lines or browsing endless aisles of goods in search of the one thing I need.

But when my oldest child, Steve, decided to flee the nest and get his own apartment, this anti-shopper had no choice. Steve was going to share rent with the son of my longtime friend, Brenda, and our boys were going to need a lot of basic necessities when they settled into their new place. So Brenda and I did what any good mother would do in this situation, besides weep and mourn the loss of her first-born—we went shopping.

Side by side, we rattled our carts down department store aisles, occasionally falling into single file when encountering other shoppers.

"You get the mop. I'll get the broom."

"Do you think they'll need a toaster?"

"They'll definitely need one of these," I said, tossing a plunger into my cart.

"What color is their kitchen?"

"Do guys even care about color coordination?"

It was then I spotted the Batman blanket. There was the Caped Crusader himself, resplendent in steely-blue-and-black polyester plush. The year that Steve turned five, Batman had posed on top of his birthday cake, ready for action. No other superhero would do. I remember searching several stores in the weeks before the big day, looking for matching paper plates, napkins and party invitations featuring the nocturnal crime fighter. For years afterward, Steve's weekly allowance often brought him another Batman comic book or action figure. Many fictional champions for justice came and went at our house, but Batman remained a constant.

Brenda joined me in the bedding aisle as I stood fingering the blanket.

"I know how you feel," she said. "I didn't think it would happen this soon."

Me, either, I thought.

It wasn't long ago that I'd knelt on the floor in a department store like this one, cradling a newborn and attempting to reason with a toddler ("Just a few more minutes! We're almost done!"), while holding up size-6 corduroys to my little boy's waist to see if they were long enough. They never were. He was growing so fast.

How many "Back-to-School" sales had I survived, navigating between displays of three-ring binders and the overloaded shopping carts of other harried parents, scavenging the bins for one last box of washable markers in basic colors?

Wasn't it yesterday that I had dragged a sullen adolescent through the young men's department, suggesting he try on some nicely pressed khakis and polo shirts in lieu of baggy jeans and T-shirts with silly slogans?

About the time Steve abandoned his fear of being seen in public with the woman who bore him, I helped him shop for his first high-school dance. We picked out the perfect shirt and tie. He looked so handsome then, so grown up—almost a man.

I didn't think it would happen so soon.

We raise our children to become self-sufficient. We do our best to guide them in developing skills to make sound judgments. If we're lucky, one day they will be ready to leave home and become independent. Then we will know we've done a good job. Still, that doesn't make it any easier to watch them go.

Brenda and I wound our way toward the checkout lanes. "This was fun," she said, squeezing my arm.

"Just a minute," I said. "I need one more thing."

I steered my cart toward the book and magazine section and scanned the shelves. Yes! There it was. I made my choice quickly, tossing it on top of the bath towels and toaster, waste can and bed sheets—offerings of love and support for a grown son who would soon learn to fend for himself.

One more Batman comic book couldn't hurt.

The Order of Things

by
Sallie Wagner Brown

After 32 years of the greatest ride I never expected to have, I spent my last morning as a fully involved mom sitting in a high school parking lot. On his 16th birthday—that threshold of independence—my son and youngest child Chris slid into my chocolate brown GMC Jimmy. He was balancing a red spiral notebook, a blue-trimmed black backpack and the remains of a banana.

Breathlessly, he asked, "Hey, did you know a whiteboard marker will shoot clear across the classroom if you restrict the air in a tube behind it?"

The look on his face made it clear he'd done just that very thing, probably along with several other adolescents more interested in the element of warfare than a lesson in physics. I loved these moments that allowed me to live again in the crazy world of teenagers, but I didn't have much longer until my window would close for good.

Knowing Mr. Canan, I felt confident there had been a learning experience somewhere in that adolescent shooting match. Despite the fun involved, I was spending too much of my time driving Chris back and forth across town every day to take Mr. Canan's class, held on a different high-school campus. I did this so Chris could experience the subject from a master.

Before I could comment, Chris continued, his tone now serious. "I heard some really scary news today."

"Oh, no! What?" I said as I pulled into traffic.

Chris didn't scare easily, so I couldn't help but imagine armed, heavily tattooed and pierced teenage boys—or even worse, girls—with mohawks and switchblades, lurking in the high-school hallways.

I glanced at him and he looked out the window, lips pressed together. Worry swept through me. But I had to keep an eye on traffic as we headed toward his home high school, where he'd finish his day.

Softly and ominously, he reported, "Richard got his driver's license." He held his serious face in place as long as he could before laughing at his "gotcha." His friend Richard often moved faster than his brain could process danger, so Chris had chosen the perfect candidate for that particular joke.

These last trips together in the car—laughing, being silly, catching up—felt precious because when I picked my son up from school later that day, we would head to the DMV so he could take his driver's test and get his license, too. It only made sense to let him use the Jimmy by himself after that, to save gas if nothing else. He was a good driver, a good kid, dependable.

And he didn't need his mother anymore.

When his older sister was born, and when I adopted his brothers and inherited my stepson, I had discovered the delightful commotion that comes with raising kids. Chris was my last one. I loved always having someone around who wanted to run out into the first snowstorm; someone willing to watch cartoons with me Saturday mornings while wrapped in blankets, sitting on the floor together eating spoonfuls of peanut butter dipped in Cocoa Puffs; someone who liked silly riddles and was actually impressed when I could solve them; and someone who would sing along with me in the car to my Beach Boys and Beatles CDs at full voice and without a trace of hesitation or embarrassment.

I loved teaching my kids exceedingly important things like how to whistle loudly with four fingers in their mouths and the lyrics to *Beans, Beans, the Musical Fruit.*

I even taught Chris to drive. One especially memorable lesson occurred alongside our driveway. Chris was alone in the car and I was outside watching him when he got the car stuck on a pile of snow.

I plodded through the snow, knocked on his window and hollered, "Put it in forward then reverse, back and forth. See if you can knock it loose."

No luck. I was about to lose my status as Yoda of the Steering Wheel when, as a Hail Mary pass, I said, "Turn the wheel hard to the right and gun it!" I stood back, just in case.

Holy traction! The car shot back from the pile of snow and pivoted exactly into position to go down the driveway.

Of course, I gave Chris a confident thumbs-up, suggesting I had known exactly what would happen all along, but I hadn't.

When he was out of sight around a tree, I did a victory dance that almost cost me my balance on the slippery slope. Chris was a foot taller than I was, but he had needed my help, and I came through in a stunningly impressive way. Whoo hoo!

Then, in the flicker of a laminator spitting out his new driver's license, I became superfluous in my son's life.

The next morning was sunny and crisp. I walked out with him to that old Jimmy. Using my I-mean-it face, I gave last-minute instructions: "Remember, no music, Frappuccinos or phone calls while you're driving."

"I know, Mom, lecture number 729." He'd recently started numbering my lectures, and the I-mean-it face had lost its effect.

"OK, smart guy. Slow down before the curve, not in it."

"Number 750." His smile made his comment funny instead of smart-alecky, but as he stood there leaning on the open car door, 6-foot 2-inches, with the shadow of a beard, my heart was breaking. Confidently, he slid behind the wheel, closed the door and started the car.

I sat on a wood-and-wrought-iron bench nestled among the rhododendrons next to the driveway and watched him back into the turnaround at the top of the drive. Moving out for college a couple of years later would be a formality. This day marked the emptying of the nest. I wasn't ready.

My youngest son—my last child—smoothly navigated the curvy hill of our driveway, paused at the bottom and surged onto the road. Not the slightest bit hesitant, he handled the SUV like he had been born to do it.

Despite the soul-deep emptiness, I couldn't help but remember the sense of freedom I had felt the first time I was off by myself in my mother's little silver Corvair. She tossed me her car keys and asked me to go get a pound of butter and some bread yeast.

I passed the threshold of adulthood and independence as I slid into the driver's seat, threw my wallet on the empty passenger seat and started the car, alone; it was just me and the road. The three blocks to Safeway felt like Route 66. The world seemed different, as if the air were more brilliant, clearer than before.

Of course, I took the long way. Of course, I drove by my friends' houses—fast, waving, almost hitting a tree. Of course, I pretended the Corvair was a Corvette and downshifted the automatic transmission until I left tiny metal pieces on a speed bump. Of course, I got that look from my mother when I returned, but she didn't make much of it. Glorious! Freedom *and* recognition of my personal right to be out in the world by myself!

I sat for a while on that bench, looking up at ancient Douglas firs, sensing harmony in the order of things, a familiar brilliance in the air. I smiled as I imagined the smile on Chris's face as he pulled into the high-school parking lot, alone in the car—maybe just a little too fast, but more under control than I had ever been.

Sallie and son Chris in a safer driving environment

Mother Nature's Misstep

by
Mary Eileen Williams

"A little bird flew into my nest and stole my heart."

I somehow discovered that saying a few days after my daughter was born. Now, some 30 years later, I cannot remember where I heard the phrase, but I will never forget the impact it had on me.

Whenever I bathed, cuddled or nursed my child, I found myself gazing down at that scrunched-up, tiny face and felt those words grab hold of my heart. Even I was amazed at how fiercely my maternal instincts took possession of my entire being and the indescribable love I felt for my baby. I adored that little bundle of joy beyond measure and blissfully gave all of my focus and energy in service to her every need. There was no doubt in my mind that she would forever be my little bird and

I, her mother hen.

The toddler years brought so many tender moments and treasured times. I eagerly bore witness to her every faltering step, applauded each new word and cheered on every fresh accomplishment. Her chubby hand grabbed hold of my two fingers, and we set out to explore our world together—mother and daughter—bonded by a deep and primal passion. "I wuv you," was our favorite and oft-repeated phrase.

When my daughter started school, I thrilled at her development and growth. She adjusted quickly, made new friends and learned the rudimentary skills of reading, writing and arithmetic with ease. She appeared especially gifted at phonics and, early on, spelled our last name accordingly: "WILY-UMZ." My focus continued to revolve around her as I became an active classroom volunteer and Brownie leader.

Yes, from my perspective, family life couldn't get much better. I knew that motherhood was my calling and that our relationship was close to perfect. I even felt somewhat sorry for mothers who had problems with their children and, when asked, was happy to give my take on child rearing.

The years passed by swiftly and pleasantly as I watched my daughter grow and mature. But then, with little prior warning and to my overwhelming shock and distress, the day of reckoning arrived. It came, moreover, with such vigorous verbal assault that it shook our little world to its very core.

In truth, my daughter and I both found ourselves on a hormonal and emotional roller coaster with plenty of twists and turns, ups and downs and big-time jars and jolts. It is a mystery to me that, in all of her wisdom, Mother Nature made such a monumental misstep in her design of the female life-cycle. How, in the name of all creation, could she have pre-destined daughters to enter puberty at precisely the same time their mothers were entering perimenopause? What a colossal blunder in celestial judgment that was!

In our case, the claws came out, and the little bird and the mother hen began pecking at each other with such ferocity that the barnyard became a battleground. We engaged in frequent bouts of squawking and squabbling and let fly with more than a few sarcastic and spiteful remarks. Each of us had her feathers ruffled, and each felt that the other was a rotten egg.

At long last, after years of alternating between biting each other's heads off and walking on eggshells, my daughter flew the coop and left for college. Although I missed her tremendously, the peace was gratefully appreciated, and distance did make the heart grow fonder. The dust and feathers settled, and the foul-tempered fowl began their journey toward reconciling and finding friendship and love as equal adults.

Numerous years have passed since those days and both of us—mother hen and little bird—have our individual interests and our own lives. The squabbles over pecking order are long gone, and we are now once more "of a feather" and joyfully flocking together whenever possible.

Yes, my daughter has grown into a lovely young woman and is now flying high and feathering her own nest. I marvel at her creativity, her daring, her compassion, her spontaneity and her calm and grace under pressure. She has created a life for herself with far greater independence and considerably more self-esteem and self-direction than I had at her age. In fact, she has many qualities to teach this old bird.

So, although my nest has been empty for many years, when I see my little bird, she still steals my heart. Her face is no longer scrunched and tiny but that of a fully grown, abundantly-competent and glorious woman. My protective mother-hen instincts have subsided and turned to great admiration for the magnificent individual she's become. And now, when we say, "I love you," as friends and equals, both of us can pronounce the "L" just fine.

Looking back, I may even have to amend my earlier sentiments. Despite all of our former bickering and strife, our relationship is now soaring to new heights. I guess, come to think of it, although her ways are truly mysterious at times, Mother Nature must have gotten it right after all!

Mother Hen and Little Bird

The End of an Era

by
T'Mara Goodsell

My son left for college, so I did something I claimed I would never do: I cleaned his room.

His was no ordinary messy room. I don't even know what happened, honestly. The cleaning issue started out as one of those "choose your battle" things, and before I knew it, I had gone AWOL to avoid the war. Somehow, I had remained ever optimistic that he would one day come to his senses and clean it.

Silly me, I thought.

You'd think I would have learned my lesson the year I announced, ever so sadly, that I wouldn't be able to kiss him goodnight unless he at least cleared a path to his bed.

"'K!" he chirped in his little voice and promptly did nothing.

"I mean it," I said, using my Voice of Doom for emphasis. "No tucking in. Ever."

"'K!'" he repeated, clearly much less fazed than I was. Oh, how I suffered, watching him climb into bed every night across that chasm of debris!

For starters, the dog slept in there, and my son didn't vacuum. Ever. Consequently, on the day of the big clean, I vacuumed what must have been the equivalent of several new dogs. The dog himself, provider of all that hair, ran from the room during the vacuuming. Who could blame him when it was clear the vacuum canister was packed with him?

I sat on the bed—on a comforter I hadn't seen since we took it out of the package years ago—and looked around at the process I had begun. It was like an archeological excavation, going back in time through the layers of one human's history.

There was the Lord-of-the-Ringish Period, which left behind remnants of various armor-clad creatures bearing abundant forms of plastic artillery. Their tiny tools and wee weapons were everywhere.

Just beneath this layer, the Legoic Era was revealed. The Legoic Era was characterized by fossils of small, multicolored snap-together blocks that made horrible noises when they got stuck in the vacuum. This era lasted the longest, so remains were easy to find, especially if one was stupid enough to walk into my son's room with bare feet.

Going down further, I found the Pokemonic Period. Very little was left from this era because of the fact that those little cards were just too darn easy to throw away.

The very bottom layer of all was the Trainish Era. Characteristic of this time period was anything whatsoever having to do with trains, especially smiley ones with British accents that used to be pop-culture icons. Sadly, little was left of the Train-ish Era besides the memories and an old engine-themed pillow shoved into the back of the closet.

On the walls were the layered outcroppings of my son's participant sports, where trophies lined dusty shelves like gilded plastic idols. Farthest back was the soccer layer. *How I remember those days!* There was the time in very early Midwest-ern spring—still winter, really—when I had shivered on the sidelines and thought I would freeze to death. I'd chattered so violently that someone's Golden Retriever had come up and licked me on the face, looking concerned. I'm sure it was try-ing to figure out where the whiskey was located. So was I.

Then there was the summer my son attended soccer camp in Savannah, Georgia. The players hosed themselves with cold water and played while soaking wet; the rest of us hunkered down in tiny pools of shade.

I was surprised to unearth a softball layer, so small I'd actu-ally forgotten about those two summers down south; I'd spent each game trying to fight off swarms of biting bugs.

Throughout it all, the Swimming Era stretched, overlap-ping with the Lifeguarding Era, leaving layers of ribbons and medals and goofy-looking broken goggles. *Can it really be over? Is it possible?*

At the bottom of the pile, I found one of those 20-ques-tion devices. The idea behind the game is to think of an object and press the "yes" or "no" buttons in response to the little ma-chine's questions until it makes the correct guess.

I sat down to rest and decided to play the game, using the mess in my son's room as my object.

"Animal?" the machine asked me. "Vegetable? Mineral?"

"Yes," I pressed.

"Bigger than a microwave?"

Each particle or taken collectively? I looked around and decided it had to be taken collectively. Like the dog hair, it was practically its own entity. *Definitely.*

"Is it dangerous?"

Yes, I thought, searching for a tissue for the umpteenth time.

I fooled the machine, which clearly had never been programmed to correctly process the globs of dust and debris in my son's room.

That made two of us.

It was the end of an era, but the beginning of a new adventure. My adventure. Clean slate and all.

T'Mara in son Tim's first college dorm room

NYMB Series Founders

Together, Dahlynn and Ken McKowen have 60-plus years of professional writing, editing, publication, marketing and public relations experience. Full-time authors and travel writers, the two have such a large body of freelance work that when they reached more than 2,000 articles, stories and photographs published, they stopped counting. And the McKowens are well respected ghostwriters, having worked with CEOs and founders of some of the nation's biggest companies. They have even ghostwritten for a former U.S. president and a few California governors and elected officials.

From 1999 to 2009, Ken and Dahlynn were consultants and coauthors for *Chicken Soup for the Soul*, where they collaborated with series founders Jack Canfield and Mark Victor Hansen on several books such as *Chicken Soup for the Entrepreneur's Soul; Chicken Soup for the Soul in Menopause; Chicken Soup for the Fisherman's Soul;* and *Chicken Soup for the Soul: Celebrating Brothers and Sisters*. They also edited and ghost-created many more Chicken titles during their tenure, with Dahlynn reading more than 100,000 story submissions.

For highly acclaimed outdoor publisher Wilderness Press, the McKowens' books include *Best of Oregon and Washington's Mansions, Museums and More; The Wine-Oh! Guide to California's Sierra Foothills* and national award-winning *Best of California's Missions, Mansions and Museums*.

Under Publishing Syndicate, the couple authored and

published *Wine Wherever: In California's Mid-Coast & Inland Region*, and are actively researching wineries for *Wine Wherever: In California's Paso Robles Region*, the second book in the Wine Wherever series.

If that's not enough, the McKowens are also the creators of the Wine Wherever iPhone mobile winery-destination journaling app and are currently creating a travel television show under the same brand (www.WineWherever.com).

Ken with his aunt Ireta (left) and mom Ruth (front) visiting the California State Fair in 2013.

Dahlynn with her mom, Scharre

Dahlynn's son, Shawn, being a typical teen

NYMB Co-Creator

About Dianna Graveman

Dianna Graveman was an unlikely candidate for mother-hood. She had no younger siblings and, as a youngster in need of spending cash, chose retail jobs over babysitting every time. Then she met the perfect guy, got married and wham! She became a mom three times in less than four years. Who'd have thought?

"Least Likely to Become a Mom" was probably also least likely to become an elementary school teacher, but that happened, too. At the ripe age of 40, armed with a newly minted bachelor's degree from the University of Missouri-St. Louis, Dianna began her second career—as a third-grade teacher.

Later, Dianna earned an MFA in writing, taught English at several area colleges and worked as a manuscript editor, corporate training designer and freelance writer and editor. Today, Dianna presents workshops and programs for writing conferences, universities, schools, corporations and business groups, in addition to providing business communications services through 2 Rivers Communications & Design and working with independent authors through Treehouse Author Services. Occasionally, she still has time to write a story or article for publication and optimistically has several book ideas under development.

And just to set the record straight, in spite of early signs to the contrary, Dianna now adores children and hopes to have a whole passel of grandkids someday. She keeps in touch with many of the moms of her former elementary school students and loves to see pictures of the kids all grown up!

Visit Dianna at www.diannagraveman.com. Follow her on Twitter: @diannagraveman.

Contributor Bios

Jenny Beatrice is an East-Coast transplant now living in St. Louis, Missouri with her husband, three children, mother, dog and rabbit. Her sense of humor, passion for writing and career in communications help to spin her family's memories and mishaps into relatable stories that point out the comedy of everyday life. Blog: correctionsandclarifications.com

Cynthia Ballard Borris is the author of *No More Bobs*, a quirky misadventure. A humor columnist, she is a former board member of the National Society of Newspaper Columnists and a frequent contributor to *Chicken Soup for the Soul, Not Your Mother's Book* and numerous publications. Contact her at cynthiaborris@gmail.com or cynthiaborris.blogspot.com.

Debra Ayers Brown is a freelance writer, blogger, magazine columnist and award-winning marketing professional. Enjoy her stories in *Not Your Mother's Books, Chicken Soup for the Soul, Guideposts, Woman's World* and more. She graduated with honors from UGA and earned her MBA from The Citadel. Please visit www.DebraAyersBrown.com and www.About.Me/DebraAyersBrown.

Sallie Wagner Brown writes about her kids who are more grown up than she, her dogs who are smarter than she, and her adventures as a traveler, teacher, writer, boater, mom and grammy. Find her stories in *Cup of Comfort, Chicken Soup for the Soul* and *Not Your Mother's Book* anthologies.

Kristen Capps has written a column on solutions to common life obstacles and she freelances articles for the *Brentwood News*. She is currently teaching high school English and has recently co-written an e-book called *Candidly Speaking: Just between Us Girls*. Visit her at www.candidlyspeaking.net.

Barbara Carpenter has three novels, two memoirs and several anthologies and articles under her belt. She is currently at work on the memoirs of a Cuban-born doctor's wife. Two children, four grandchildren and two great-grandsons—one an infant—keep her busy. Barbara sees writing as icing on a very sweet cake.

Candace Carrabus writes stories and rides horses—frequently simultaneously! Her books, published by Witting Woman Works, including *Raver, The Horsecaller: Book One* and *On the Buckle, Dreamhorse Mystery #1* are at Amazon, Barnes & Noble and Kobo. She loves visitors! Knock on her door anytime at www.candacecarrabus.com or www.facebook.com/AuthorCandaceCarrabus.

Kathryn Cureton writes from the basement lair of her hillbilly mansion in southeast Missouri. She makes a living teaching high school science. Her hobbies include bragging that she graduated valedictorian, keeping her husband from using the front yard sinkhole as nature's giant wastebasket and using prepositions to end sentences with.

Shari Courter married her high school sweetheart, Ron, in 1993. They have one son, Zac, and three daughters—Aubrey, Kearstin and Caymen. Shari is a stay-at-home mom, a licensed massage therapist and a Zumba instructor. In her spare time, she enjoys blogging about her family's antics at CloseCourters.Blogspot.com.

Terri Elders lives near Colville, Washington with a dog and three cats. A lifelong writer and editor, her stories have appeared in dozens of periodicals and anthologies. She's a co-creator for *Not Your Mother's Book. . . On Travel* and the upcoming *On Sharing Secrets* and *My First Time*. She blogs at atouchoftarragon.blogspot.com.

Melissa Face lives in southeastern Virginia and enjoys traveling to New England with her family. She teaches high school English and writes when she's not grading student work. Melissa is currently pregnant with her second child; she hasn't received nearly as many gestation citations this time around. Email: writermsface@yahoo.com

Pamela Frost lives in Port St. Lucie, Florida. Her award-winning debut novel, *Houses of Cards* (available on Amazon and Kindle), is the story of a family who tried to get rich quick in real estate and its hilarious misadventures. She is the co-creator of *NYMB...On Home Improvement*.

Marcia Gaye is a poet, memoirist, songwriter and author of cross-genre nonfiction and fiction. She currently lives in St. Charles, Missouri with her husband. Her two children have grown up to be a teacher/musician and an advocate for students with special needs. Marcia's publications and contact information can be found at www.marciagaye.com.

Catherine Giordano is a public speaker, writer, blogger and poet living in Orlando, Florida. Her books include *The Poetry Connection; What Ifs, If Onlys, and So Whets*; and *News Print Poetry 2012*. Her stories and poetry have been published in several magazines and anthologies. Catherine's website is www.talksallabout.com.

T'Mara Goodsell is an award-winning multi-genre writer and teacher who lives near St. Louis, Missouri. She has written for various anthologies, newspapers and publications and is currently working on a book for young adults. More of her writing can be found at http://messageinbloggletheartofbeingbroken.blogspot.com.

Laura Graf is the mother of four and a former teacher with a background in early childhood. Currently, she is working on a picture book for children, as well as co-authoring a book titled *Ride to Redemption* with T R Freeman. She enjoys writing, painting, camping and spending time with family.

Ellie Grossman is an award-winning writer and speaker whose book, *Mishegas of Motherhood: Raising Children To Leave The Nest . . . As Long As They Come Home For Dinner,* combines satire with Jewish wisdom for modern families. She is co-producer/director of "Listen To Your Mother," a national movement to give Mother's Day a microphone.

Stacey Gustafson is a featured writer for the Erma Bombeck Writers' Workshop. She has a blog called "Are You Kidding Me?" based on her suburban family and everyday life. Her stories appear in *Chicken Soup for the Soul* and *NYMB... On Being a Woman, Travel, Parent* and *Home Improvement.* Blog: www.staceygustafson.com, Twitter: @mepaint

Erika Hoffman is a former teacher, a position for which she was certified and paid. In addition to that labor of love, she's also served in the unpaid and untrained roles of caregiver, mother and dog sitter. Erika writes nonfiction for anthologies, magazines, ezines and newspapers. Occasionally, she publishes mysteries!

Mary Horner is the author of *Strengthen Your Nonfiction Writing.* She teaches communications at St. Louis and St. Charles Community Colleges and is the former managing editor of the *Journal of the American Optometric Association.* Mary blogs at www.writrteachr.blogspot.com.

Georgia Hubley retired from financial management after 20 years to write full time. Vignettes of her life have been published in *Woman's World, Chicken Soup for the Soul,* the *Hallmark* book series and other anthologies and periodicals. Two grown sons have left the nest; she resides with her husband in Henderson, Nevada.

Renee Hughes previously had a humorous story appear in *Not Your Mother's Book...On Dogs.* She is a CPA and lives with her hubby and rescued bunny in St. Louis, Missouri. She also has two grown children. Interests include writing, acoustic guitar, church activities and indie/alternative music. www.squirrelb8.com

Georgia Mellie Justad's humorous writings have appeared in *The Storyteller* and *ParentingPlus,* as well as numerous other publications. A transplanted Southern belle, this Georgia native resides in South Florida, or what she fondly calls "The

Land of the Southern Impaired," with her husband and son. Visit her at www.possumqueenscene.wordpress.com.

Mary-Lane Kamberg is a professional writer in Olathe, Kansas. She has two daughters and the three smartest, cutest grandchildren on the face of the earth. She specializes in writing nonfiction for school libraries. She is co-leader of the Kansas City Writers Group and author of *The "I Don't Know How To Cook" Book*.

Nancy Julien Kopp writes creative nonfiction, memoir, inspirational, poetry, award-winning children's fiction and articles on the writing craft. She's published in 13 *Chicken Soup for the Soul* books, other anthologies, newspapers, ezines and Internet radio. She blogs about the writing world with tips for writers at www.writergrannysworld.blogspot.com.

Liane Kupferberg Carter is a journalist whose articles and essays have appeared in many publications, including *The New York Times*, the *Chicago Tribune* and the *Huffington Post*. She writes a monthly column for *Autism After 16* and is currently completing a memoir. You can follow her at www.huffingtonpost.com/liane-kupferberg-carter.

Lisa McManus Lange writes slice-of-life stories from Victoria, BC, Canada. Her stories can be found in other *Not Your Mother's Book*s, as well as in *Chicken Soup for the Soul* books. Find her at www.lisamcmanuslange.blogspot.com and lisamc2010@yahoo.ca.

Mary Laufer is a freelance writer and substitute teacher in Saint Cloud, Florida. Her essays, short stories and poems have been published in magazines, newspapers and more than 30 anthologies, including *NYMB...On Being a Parent, Chicken Soup for the Soul*, and *A Shaker of Margaritas: A Bad Hair Day*.

Rebecca MacKenzie, a prize-winning essayist and *NYMB* alumnus (*On Being a Stupid Kid*), writes from her home in Oconomowoc, Wisconsin. Her work appears in teaching, writing, parenting and religious publications. An early childhood educator, she enjoys developing curriculum. Foremost, Rebecca is wife to Ken and mother to Elyssa and Daniel.

Debra Mayhew is a pastor's wife and home-schooling mom to seven (usually) sweet children. After faith and family, her greatest passion is writing. Debra has had several short stories and children's poems published and is currently at work on a middle-grade novel. Visit her at www.debramayhew.com.

Madeline McEwen is an ex-pat from the UK, bifocaled and technically challenged. Together with her Significant Other, they currently enjoy fragile custody of three minors and a major—two with autism, two without—and a time-share with Alzheimer's when life gets too crazy. Visit http://www.blogger.com/profile/05828186178060722812.

Laurel McHargue graduated from USMA in 1983. Her constant quest for adventure landed her in Leadville, Colorado, where she currently writes and resides with her husband and her German Shepherd. She recently published her first novel, *Miss?* and has co-created *Not Your Mother's Book...On Being a Stupid Kid*. She blogs at www.leadvillelaurel.com.

Kelly Melang, a self-made trophy wife, writes humor from Winston Salem and Beech Mountain, North Carolina. Married to Jeff, Kelly enjoys all outdoor sports with her sons, Wolfgang and Max. "It's all about making people laugh—the louder the better." You can follow her blog, "That Grey Area," at www.blueridgeandrv.blogspot.com.

Lesley Morgan is an art educator, visual artist, author and mother of four boys. Her previously published work includes poems, work-related nonfiction and stories in *Not Your Mother's Book...On Home Improvement*. She lives near the New Hampshire seacoast.

Jan Morrill's award-winning short stories have been published in *Chicken Soup for the Soul* and other anthologies. Her debut novel, *The Red Kimono*, was published by The University of Arkansas Press (February 2013). She enjoys speaking at events and is working on the sequel to *The Red Kimono*. www.janmorrill.com.

Amy Mullis embarrasses her children from her home in the Sweet Tea Section of South Carolina. She earned an Honorable Mention in the Erma Bombeck Writing Competition and has served up essays in a buffet of anthologies. For more "Don't Let This Happen To Me" moments, visit her blog, MindoverMullis.com.

Alice Muschany lives in Wentzville, Missouri. Her hobbies include writing, photography and spoiling her grandchildren. Her stories have been published in *Cup of Comfort, Chicken Soup, Guideposts* and *Not Your Mother's Book*. She is also a popular opinion shaper for the local magazine *Suburban Journal*. Contact her at aliceandroland@gmail.com.

Amanda Mushro is a mommy of two who blogs at *Questionable Choices in Parenting*. Sometimes she thinks she is doing a great job as a mom, but then she does something that really makes her question her own parenting abilities. Find her at QuestionableChoicesInParenting.com.

Eva Lesko Natiello is a writer and freelance communications and marketing professional. She blogs humor pieces and parenting stories. Her debut suspense novel, *The Memory Box*, is forthcoming. Eva improvises songs as a way to dialogue with her kids. They infrequently find it entertaining. Visit her at: www.evanatiello. com and http://connect.nj.com/user/EvaLeskoNatiello/posts.html.

Pat Nelson, writer, editor and workshop presenter on anthologies and on finding your story, is co-creator of *NYMB...On Being a Parent* and two upcoming titles: *On Being a Grandparent* and *On Working for a Living*. Her stories appear in *The Valley Bugler* and at www.LewisRiver.com. Visit her at www.Storystorm.US.

Linda O'Connell has proof that she survived motherhood—her kids have given her laugh lines. She is a multi-published writer and co-creator of *Not Your Mother's Book...On Family*. Linda enjoys teaching preschoolers, strolling on the beach and eating dark chocolate. She blogs at http://lindaoconnell.blogspot.com.

Suzanne Olsen's humor essays have appeared in *The Oregonian* and *Not Your Mother's Book...On Home Improvement*. She's co-written articles about solar energy for *Home Power* magazine and edited the book *Footprint, A Funny Thing Happened on the Way to Extinction,* about global warming. Visit her at www.suzanneolsen.com and www.gentlehumor.com.

Lucia Paul's humor writing includes an award-winning sitcom script and essays that have appeared in numerous publications. She is also a contributor to *NYMB... On Home Improvement*. When she's not working on her upcoming humor collection, *Home Buyers Just Aren't That Into You,* she's not working out.

Jill Pertler touches hearts and funny bones with her weekly syndicated column, "Slices of Life," printed in 130 newspapers across the U.S. She is a playwright, author of *The Do-it-Yourselfer's Guide to Self-Syndication* and has stories in four *Chicken Soup* books and *NYMB...On Home Improvement*. Follow *Slices of Life* on Facebook.

Elizabeth Philip earned a bachelor of social work and a master of arts in teaching. She currently teaches composition and literature in Missouri. Residing with her husband, two children and three dogs, she spends her free time reading, cooking gourmet meals and gardening.

Emily Rich is a former federal employee and community college instructor who, after being diagnosed with both autoimmune arthritis and cancer, decided to take some time off to write. She lives in Arlington, Virginia and volunteers for the literary magazine *Little Patuxent Review*.

Sioux Roslawski is mother to Virginia and Ian, mother-in-law to Jason and grammy to Riley. (She's been waiting to play "grammy" for years!) A St. Louis third-grade teacher, Sioux writes in her spare time. Her writing can be found in a number of anthologies, as well as at http://siouxspage.blogspot.com.

Shayla Seay, a recent empty-nester because her son just enlisted in the military, is now the full-time mother to a dog named Taz and a cat named Kramer.

Terri Spilman is a writer living by the mantra, "At least it will make a good story." Her work is published in *Not Your Mother's Book...On Being a Woman*, the *Current in Carmel* and *Hamilton County Family* magazine. She also writes humor essays and commentary in her blog, thelaughingmom.wordpress.com.

Camille Subramaniam lives in Missouri, loves her family and writes during the baby's naptime. The Northwest Houston RWA named her debut novel, *Voodoo Butterfly*, a 2013 Lone Star contest finalist. Camille's stories are inspired by her travels to 27 countries and counting! Follow her journey at www.camillefaye.com.

Roselie Thoman is a mother, writer and educator. She lives in the Pacific Northwest with her husband and two children. After the traumatic first go-around with her daughter, Cali, she successfully potty trained her son in two days, after taking the sound and simple advice of one person.

Angela Thomas is an intuitive consultant, instructor and writer. Currently, she teaches writing at a university, as well as operates a small company, Affinity Entertainment Productions. Thomas has an MFA in writing and has published a variety of fiction, nonfiction and prose. For more information, visit www.affinity-entertainmentproductions.com and www.angelathomas.org.

Lisa Tognola, a freelance writer who pens the blog Mainstreetmusingsblog.com, highlights the humorous side of suburban life—the good, the bad and the ugly. She is the parenting and lifestyles contributor at Manilla.com and contributes to the online magazine More.com. Twitter: @lisatognola.

Donna Volkenannt believes stories have the power to inspire, uplift and heal. The first place winner of the 2012 Erma Bombeck Global Humor Award, Donna lives in Missouri, where she blogs about writing and the sweet mysteries of life. Visit her at http://donnasbookpub.blogspot.com.

Pat Wahler is a grant writer by day and writer of fiction and essays by night. Her work is published in both national and local venues. A lifelong animal lover, Pat ponders critters, writing and life's little mysteries at www.critteralley.blogspot.com.

Kristi Stephens Walker is a former reporter, editor and proofreader. Currently, she freelances as a writer and blogs about funny stuff that happens to regular women. You can read her blog at www.nosissyrodeo.blogspot.com. She is currently working on her first novel.

Dawn Weber's essays have been published in several humor anthologies. She won a National Society of Newspaper Columnists humor award for her newspaper column. She's finishing her first book of essays and resides in Ohio with her family and an ever-changing series of ill-mannered pets. Visit Dawn at lightenupweber. blogspot.com.

Dacia Wilkinson is the wife of a biker, mother of six and is a trade-school instructor, where she plays at teaching psychology and English composition. She feels blessed to teach subjects she loves. Dacia enjoys writing and creating characters and has penned three novels, with one more on the way. www.daciawilkinson.wordpress.com

Christy Lynne Williams lives in Arizona with her husband and their two other knights in shining armor. She pulls her stories from her experiences as a stay-at-home-mom and has shared her highs and lows in two anthologies, as well as her blog: iamstilltheprincess.blogspot.com.

Mary Eileen Williams is the founder/host of the popular blog and radio show *Feisty Side of Fifty* (www.feistysideoffifty.com). A longtime career coach with a master's degree in career development, she is the author of the book *Land the Job You Love* and writes job-search articles for the *Huffington Post*.

Linda Wolff shares her adventures from carpool to empty nest on her lifestyle blog www.CarpoolGoddess.com. Her work has been featured on *Huffington Post*, *Scary Mommy*, Erma Bombeck Writers' Workshop and many others. She loves carbs, disco, her family and online shopping, in various order. Tweet her at @carpoolgoddess.

Story Permissions

Holey Moley © 2013 Jenny R. Beatrice
Ma's in the Cupboard © 2004 Cynthia Borris
A Change of Tune © 2013 Debra Brown
The Order of Things © 2010 Sallie Wagner Brown
Mommy Wars © 2012 Kristen Capps
One and the Same © 2013 Barbara Carpenter
A Most Appropriate Moment © 2013 Liane Kupferberg Carter
Pavlov's Dogs and Potty Training © 2010 Shari Courter
The Consummate Performer © 2012 Kathryn Cureton
Baby-Book Bloopers © 2009 Theresa J. Elders
Gestation Citations © 2010 Melissa Face
A Bucket Full © 2006 Pamela Frost
A Mother's Expectations © 2012 Marcia S. Gaye
The Accidental Kidnapper © 2013 Catherine Giordano
The End of an Era © 2009 T'Mara Goodsell
An Unforgettable Gaffe © 2013 Laura Graf
So Long to Superheroes © 2006 Dianna Graveman
The ABCs of ACTs © 2013 Ellie Grossman
Class Clown © 2013 Stacey Gustafson
Keeping It Real © 2011 Erika Hoffman
The Tooth Fairy's Bad Rep © 2011 Mary E. Horner
Learning to Fly © 2007 Georgia Hubley
Grazing Crazy O's © 2013 Renee A. Hughes
Amen, Shucks © 2005 Georgia Melinda Justad
Kill the Wabbit © 2013 Georgia Melinda Justad
Buen Provecho! © 1995 Mary-Lane Kamberg
Off the Hook © 2013 Nancy Julien Kopp
Rules © 2013 Lisa Lange
Empty House © 2008 Mary Laufer
Balancing Act © 2013 Rebecca Lynn MacKenzie
Throwing in the Towel © 2013 Debra Mayhew
Second Time Around © 2013 Madeline McEwen
No Trampoline Time © 2014 Laurel J. McHargue
Measuring Up © 2013 Dahlynn McKowen

Publishing Syndicate

Publishing Syndicate LLC is an independent book publisher based in Northern California. The company has been in business for more than a decade, mainly providing writing, ghostwriting and editing services for major publishers. In 2011, Publishing Syndicate took the next step and expanded into a full-service publishing house.

The company is owned by married couple Dahlynn and Ken McKowen. Dahlynn is the CEO and publisher, and Ken serves as president and managing editor.

Publishing Syndicate's mission is to help writers and authors realize personal success in the publishing industry, and, at the same time, provide an entertaining reading experience for its customers. From hands-on book consultation and their very popular and free monthly *Wow Principles* publishing tips e-newsletter to forging book deals with both new and experienced authors and launching three new anthology series, Publishing Syndicate has created a powerful and enriching environment for those who want to share their writing with the world. (www.PublishingSyndicate.com)

NYMB Needs Your Stories!

We are looking for hip, fun, modern and very-much-today type stories, just like those in this book, for 30 new titles in the *NYMB* series. Published contributors are compensated.

Submission guidelines at www.PublishingSyndicate.com

We Need Stories!

Submission guidelines at www.PublishingSyndicate.com

We Need Stories!

Not Your Mother's Book... On Menopause
65 stories about that freakin' change of life
Edited by Dahlynn McKowen, Ken McKowen and Stacey Hatton

Not Your Mother's Book... On Embarrassing Moments
65 hilarious stories about life's most awkward moments
Edited by Dahlynn McKowen, Ken McKowen and Pamela Frost

Not Your Mother's Book... On Working for a Living
65 stories by working stiffs
Edited by Dahlynn McKowen, Ken McKowen and Pat Nelson

Not Your Mother's Book... On Senior Moments
65 hilarious stories about aging gracefully
Edited by Dahlynn McKowen and Ken McKowen

Not Your Mother's Book... On Sharing Secrets
65 stories, many told for the very first time
Edited by Dahlynn McKowen, Ken McKowen and Terri Elders

Available Now!

Stand Up! is THE generation-defining book that focuses on the global youth movement. Seventy-five of the world's most dynamic young activists share their amazing experiences and challenge readers through spirited calls to action. By way of their grassroots movements and international work, these young people are bringing their own brand of savvy compassion and unstoppable courage to the crossroads of social enterpreneurship and activism.

Edited and introduced by John Schlimm

The Cow-Pie Chronicles follows 10-year-old Tim Slinger and his annoying little sister Dana as they grow up on their family dairy farm. Join Tim on his many crazy adventures--from teasing a bull to building forts in the hayloft--and learn about the re-alities of life on a farm, including the hard work required of Tim and Dana to take care of teh land and their farm animals.

Author: James Butler
Illustrator: Lonnie Millsap

Order both from your favorite book retailer today!